HAROLD AND THE ACID SEA
OF REALITY

Doug Rucker
Layout by Helane Freeman

Doug Rucker
Vilimapubco
Malibu, CA
ruckerdoug@gmail.com

Printed in the United States of America

Library of Congress Control Number: 2016935561

ISBN 978-0-9968060-2-2

First Edition
10 9 8 7 6 5 4 3 2 1

CONTENTS

FORWARD

Write rhymes with right and helps me remember it seems right to write because I get to enjoy my thoughts as I think them. They stay with me as long as I save them on my computer. I date them and know what I've thought at a certain time. Later, when in a reading mode, I'm able to experience them again with a fresh eye and fresh mind. Eventually they freeze into place and take a stand within myself as either good, mediocre or bad. Of course, I'm the only one required to know which. Always to write is always to record, always to re-think, always to revise and learn. I have things to put down, I'm in the generative mood. It's fun!

Thinking things clearly enough to write them down enables me to solidify my thoughts. My state of conviction or lack of it when I write becomes more pronounced when I put words and thoughts down on paper. Though subject to change at all times, more solid convictions allow me to know my better point of view, and while continuing to keep an open mind and valuing change, I have a growing knowledge about where I stand and what I believe. Writing gives me a sense of assurance that is useful as a platform upon which to make other quantitative, and if necessary, changeable leaps.

It's my true belief that *the greatest adventures lie within the realm of my own personal ignorance.* That is, great adventures lie in new knowledge and new feelings. However I phrase it, it's my plan to advance vigorously into that unknown territory; my own ignorance.

Harold and the Acid Sea of Reality is essays, poems, dreams and thoughts, both humorous and serious, that have flown from my mind and are hereby recorded. Whether for enjoyment or reference, at least I know where they are - between the covers of this book:

Harold and the Acid Sea of Reality

HAROLD
AND THE ACID SEA OF
REALITY

HAROLD AND THE ACID SEA OF REALITY
(Harold comes to find himself)

Harold finds himself high in the sky floating above the clouds and more or less happy. He's contented in the clouds and cooled by drifting breezes. Unmarried, he lives in FANTASY and though believing in free love and encouraged by the opposite sex, is too shy to act. He has places to go and things to do; movies, TV, surfing, lunch with buddies, or other partially-fulfilling activities.

Healthy, he has a reasonable job but prefers instant gratification such as a chocolate sundae, watching the game, or taking off for Monday morning at the beach. There are no threatening aspects in his life, no sharks circling for the kill, no pack of wolves waiting to pounce, no mortal accidents about to occur, and except for a few frightening dreams, Harold assumes his life is better than most and mildly happy, he lolls in the clouds.

What Harold doesn't understand is that he is accompanied by three things hidden under his skin and part of his being; an alarming dark patch under each of his arms we might call THE PAIN OF THE SCOLDING PARENT. It criticizes him at the most disadvantageous of times. And a circular shape covering his heart and larynx called THE CHILD WITHIN who enjoys life when he likes it and is furious when he doesn't. Then there's the round sphere just behind his navel called THE WAITING ADULT. It's about to come of age and is not completely developed. If THE <u>WAITING</u> ADULT were THE <u>FOUND</u> ADULT, Harold would become the person the Universe always intended him to be.

Until now Harold had assumed he was happy in his life of FANTASY, but his mind has been filled with mental vacations, life on a South Seas island with gently swaying palm trees, perfect surf, and a beautiful woman telling him how much he's adored. But at present he continues to focus on FANTASY and doesn't know he's already begun to fall from his great height.

> *For in the evening*
> *Starlight whispers softly.*
> *Calls to me in pussy willow tones*
> *That reach my middle mind*
> *And blow cool zephyrs*
> *Across the shallows of my heart.*
> *I know you mind,*
> *And you, feather-softened thoughts*
> *That yield not*
> *But as the stone,*
> *Press their burning way.*
> *Come to me, sweet one,*
> *You, with smiling eye.*
> *Linger softly in my soul*
> *And cover me with lemon-love.*

Harold's middle mind has finally reached *the feather-softened thoughts that yield not but press their burning way,* the first indication of a major shift in viewpoint. We've all heard, *"When the chips are down, the only thing truly changeable is your own attitude."* Harold was facing that vital transition.

At various times, doing normal things, he'd sweat

droplets of fear and his friends, not willing to lose a close buddy, attempted to keep him aloft. But fate had spoken. The time was right. A correction was in order. That comfortable balance of existence, Yin and Yang, was a bit one-sided. Noticing he's not quite the same, his friends and relatives tried to help him return to the sky. But all lasting relationships are dynamic, and if one changes, all must change.

His CHILD WITHIN issued heart-rending cries and feared the change. The SCOLDING PARENT, sensing something different, reproached, admonished, and criticized all solutions. Both were unhappy, since they had noticed the impending revision and wanted Harold to continue in the customary circles and to remain his familiar, former self. Harold partly capitulated because he wanted to remain aloft, but could no longer avoid hearing the wind whistling past his ears and noticing he'd already dropped well below the clouds. And soon, in desperate fear of the grim reaper, he fell like the wind while THE ACID SEA OF REALITY swiftly advanced to meet him.

Shooting in the air like military explosions, he splashed into THE ACID SEA OF REALITY! Seagulls took to the sky, waves surged across the ocean in steady mounds reaching Hawaii and setting off the emergency tsunami alert, and THE WHITE BIRD OF ENLIGHTENMENT, impervious to natural conditions, came to rest on top of his head to do her work.

Hitting the water was painful to Harold and THE SCOLDING PARENT said, *"I told you so!"* The CHILD WITHIN is shocked, frightened and furious, and momentarily distanced himself from THE WAITING ADULT. THE WAITING ADULT, dropping on him like a hopeful disease, felt a mixed sense of relief and the damaged FANTASY broke apart in small pieces and began to dissolve. For you see,

THE ACID SEA IS REALITY

Once below the silvery surface, Harold slowly sinks from the brightness through the ever-darkening ACID water to eventually settle in the blackness and murkiness of the seemingly hopeless brown muck.

To murk along in the sea
beneath the dim waters
and think that above
the glimmering surface,
the sky, clouds, breeze
could sweep him
into arms of angels.
But there he is stuck,
pinned and wriggling,
squirming like a rat
impaled on a prong.
Even yet,
he knows it's there.
He feels its call,
its urgency,
it's all life.
But his every effort
mires more deeply
his being.
You know,
I know,
everyone knows
but Harold,
to live is to LET GO!

The word ACID symbolizes the difficulty in dealing with Harold's SCOLDING PARENT and it was necessary for him to go inward and examine why he finds himself at the bottom of the ACID SEA and stuck in the mud. After searching for months, he finds it necessary to remember his early childhood and to examine how his parents brought him up. He asked himself who they were and how they got that way. Surprisingly, he finds he was taught both good and bad things. What worked, he kept. What didn't, he should have discarded. Then he discovered he needed to recount the lives of his grandparents to see how his parents were raised and how they became who they were, for they were the ones who raised him. He did so and discovered, *"OH! That's why his grandparents were that way! And OH! That's why my parents were that way. And OH! That's how I got that way."*

Harold absorbs the new knowledge with the help of the WHITE BIRD OF ENLIGHTENMENT who continued to do her work, and which with difficulty allowed him to dog paddle in the pain-laden ACID SEA. The SCOLDING PARENT, praised be our infinite God, moved to FANTASY LAND never to return.

His real self, his HEARTSORE, appears:

Once dragged from its hiding place,
we see its countenance, weak, slithery,
frightened of the bright lights,
fearful, ugly in the sun,
out of place and unable to return.
What shall we do with it?
What will it do by itself?
It is lost. It is big.
It needs care and feeding.
It seems to have weight and mass,
but no sense of how to cope.
It must be dried, spoon-fed and taught.

It must come to be tanned by the sun.
It must develop calluses by working.
Its eyes are watery
and its vision is distorted.
We must dry its eyes
so that it can see clearly.
We have to work the fat off it
to see if it can be something.
It is ugly in its rebirth,
but we don't know what it is yet.
It must use itself to see what it will be.
It leaves spots on the pavement.
It is big and unused.
Just looking at it,
it seems to have potential,
but until it does something,
we will not know what.
A lot of energy must be expended
especially at first.

After months of hard work asking and answering difficult questions, THE SCOLDING PARENT, began to relinquish power to Harold's WAITING ADULT who was delighted to move forward into a position of greater power. THE CHILD WITHIN, gaining confidence, began to look to THE WAITING ADULT for assurance. Harold absorbed new knowledge and allowing HOPE to quietly enter his mind, he began to see there is much more to REALITY than FANTASY. The symbols, YIN and YANG, became more evenly balanced. The strengthened ADULT practiced controlling and developing power to ward off accidents, troubles and most problems and then the appearance of THE CHILD WITHIN:

I say to the boy,
"How are you, boy?"
He looks at me
with open eyes
as if to ask,
"Who are you?
And why do you wish to know?"
I smile an easy smile,
take off my hat,
and with handkerchief
so slightly soiled,
I wipe my brow
and uneasily, I say,
"You are my own,
the one I love,
the boy I've kept
as part of me
for, lo, these years.
The one I've longed to hold
so close within my arms
until the days and hours
of all the time
whereof we've lost
shall come to catch us
once again
and we are filled to overflowing
with love, glowing."

THE CHILD WITHIN enjoys being known by his old but formerly hidden companion. THE GROWING ADULT suggested places to go, things to do. In the light of REALITY, things looked different. Harold understood and forgave himself and his parents. He claimed his space.

To stop the struggle
means an upward float.
With great strength
and stillness of will,
he ceases to struggle
and slowly, meekly,
gently, rises to the surface,
the surface and the idea.
Toward the bright light rising,
effortlessly rising,
like a blowfish, brown and prickly,
like a lovely toad ascending
through the muck.
Like a painted eye
with a willingness to open,
he lifts and rises, quiescent still,
will gently nudge the surface,
and there, as if to see the face of God,
will dare to look.

Newly strengthened in his waiting ADULT and keeping the good things left by his SCOLDING PARENT, the dark patches lightened beneath each arm and became a human truth. The silent circle of The CHILD WITHIN, now delighted with a trustworthy friend, merged with the sphere of the TRUE ADULT no longer the WAITING ADULT, who listened mindfully to suggestions of the CHILD WITHIN on places to go, things to do. Harold began to swim in THE ACID SEA OF REALITY.

From the life of lethargy withdrawn.
From the gnawing apathy he comes
to nudge the surface of the light,
the mind, the vision,

the idea.
At the surface, face to face,
and looking only,
for eagerness would blinding be,
destroying his ability,
to perceive.

Within the circle of the CHILD WITHIN, now merged with the sphere of the intelligently protective, child-affirming ADULT, Harold's YIN–YANG symbol is now perfectly balanced. He has a passionate, imaginative, adult-affirming CHILD and the motivating power of his HEART to accompany him through life. In the close distance there is someone to love and his TRUE ADULT can now swim in the NOT SO ACID SEA OF REALITY and he can go on the wonderful trips of his heart's desire.

And so it passed,
Harold slowly merged
with flowing grain
and window panes
and sunlight on a smiling house,
and children's laughter in the wind.
He came to merge with the living presence
from the tepid sea arisen,
by a welcome stranger's hand uplifted,
came to look at you and me.

FACE OF GOD

Why are you trapped behind those bars, my friend?
   I trapped myself.
A novel idea. But, to what gain?
   This way, I do not have to see the face of God.
I see. And is that so bad, the face of God?
   I don't know, I have never seen Him.
Look, then!
   Are you God!?
No.
   I don't know where to look.
Why don't you want to see the face of God?
   I am afraid He will demand something of me.
And if he does?
   I shall not be able to give it.
Why not?
   He wants my only heart.
And can you not open it to Him?
   No.
Why not?
   I have closed it forever.
Why so?
   If I open it, I shall see the face of Death.
And is that so bad, the face of Death?
   Yes.
Then you are afraid to see the face of God,
because He may require you to open your heart,
and if you do, you shall see the face of Death!
   Yes.
You stand here, then, afraid of God and Death.
   Yes.
A limbo state.
   Yes.
Afraid of God and Death.
   Yes.

THE WHOLE IDEA

(In this short essay, Harold expresses his basic feeling about his place in the world. He's tried to believe otherwise, but to no avail. He seems at this time and until further knowledge to be stuck with this viewpoint.)

I think the whole idea of a beautiful planet spinning all alone in a black void is a brutal, ruthless idea! And in four and a half billion years the planet earth has managed to get a thin ozone layer of gas that protects all that lives on the surface; plants, animals, fish, reptiles, insects, birds, man and everything else. There are millions and billions and trillions of stars in the Universe. In the center of galaxies, word has it, there are black holes where a teaspoonful of black hole matter would weigh more than ten thousand suns. Other stars explode, comets glide endlessly through eternity, and our planet, our precious little watery planet, spins on its axis with its thin, gaseous ozone and huge orbiting moon, both rotating around an average, but oh-so-important sun.

So what if our earth and sun blow up? Happens all the time. I can imagine an intelligent being far away on another planet who <u>knows</u> how many planets there are. He knows they surround us by the zillions *(true, they are light years away)* but there, on the interstellar news he hears that one planet, earth, blew itself up a half-hour ago. No survivors. *(Probably hearing this just after a soap commercial.)* But of course, he knows there are many planets in the universe dying all the time. Big deal! He knows it's doubtful there will be an overpopulation of stars or planets, for the universe is self-regulating, there being a finite amount of matter coming and going. If one section of the universe gets overcrowded, stars fall into each other and explode into gas that forms galaxies and solar systems, or they implode and form black holes. He knows the quest of the universe is for stability, dependability and growth, as well as wildness, life and death.

Do I think the pieces of earth *(and fragments of arms and legs)* are lost and gone forever? No, sir! They are temporarily out in the cold *(-450 degrees Centigrade)* and eventually will wind up as part of something else. One planet blowing up in a billion, quad-trillion years makes little difference.

But, says another, what if our beautiful planet is the only one among all the stars we see through our telescopes? *(By the way, there are so many stars to be seen through one view of even the simplest telescopes, they look like dense fog.)* There are an *INCONCEIVABLE* number of stars out there. Yes, folks, it's a starry gas out there.

Now, supposing we live on the *only* planet in the universe of gas or stars we see on a clear night. I say to you, to have something this beautiful and this rare to use and enjoy all at the same time makes losing it *REAL* poignant. I'd be *SO* sorry, folks, you can't believe it.

Finally, this universal starry gas from other stars' explosions makes us a beautiful life-supporting planet and gives it a thin atmosphere that protects and enables all life. Then one species, man *(in some ways the idiot-species of all time),* makes a bomb to blow up all living creatures including us. But, this intellectually over-developed man is capable of miracles, too, because he/she can discover DNA, make rocket ships that go to Mars and eliminate disease, while at the same time inventing bombs to blow up the planet.

If I was God and had decided on a hands-off policy and wanted to play observer and just see what man would do, I'd speculate three things: *(1)* He'll blow it up. *(2)* He'll make the planet awfully sick. *(3)* He'll opt for his own and the planet's life and not blow it up and pull a save.

Of course, I'm not God. If I were, I'd slap man up the side of the head and tell him to *"Get it together!"* But then I wonder, why is man <u>not</u> together? Why does man, being part God himself, seem not to be in control of himself? Then, I look around and see that most everything is *NOT* in control of itself. I cleaned up a mess of ants on the sink yesterday. The ants had no control over their instinct to hunt for food in my sink. Agent Orange defoliated the Vietnam trees, and after the war, exposed people were mortally affected. Trees and people had no control in Vietnam. In India, 2,000 people suddenly died because poison gas mysteriously leaked from earth. Victims had no control.

Eventually I came to the conclusion that man, as we know him, cannot control himself or much of anything. I've looked back in history for a time when he did control himself and have discovered he never controlled himself. He never controlled his anger, greed, revenge or amount of education, and as long as man is here, the Planet will be infested with *man's* disease.

Of course, the U. S. did send wheat to Africa, and we do seem to be a freer people than in the past, and brilliant people do win the Nobel Peace Prize. What the world needs is a paradigm shift.

Let us pray.

THE REALM

(The title, <u>The Realm</u> has a poetic ring, don't you think?
And Harold has a particular tale to tell in a prose-poetry
sort of way. In it he leaves out details, but only
describes the three most meaningful shades of life.
I'll let him tell it.)

I walked onto a bluff overlooking the ocean and was dumbfounded when I saw a door standing with absolutely nothing around it. It was in the middle of a meadow singled out against the horizon. Just a freestanding door in open space. And a medieval door, at that, made of weather-beaten planks, bound tight with iron hoops. It had an iron handle with no lock and a burnt message on the front that said,

"The Greatest Adventures Lie Within the Realm of Your Own Personal Ignorance."

I thought it a curious saying. On the back I found another message. It read, *"To a Richer Life."* I was sane when I left home and now I was surely as sound. I'd been hiking a trail through the woods since early morning and by noon had reached the grassy bluffs with the sea beyond. It was a good day with fair-weather clouds as far as the eye could see; the air fresh and slightly salted. But then the freestanding door and its puzzling title, *The Greatest Adventures Lie Within the Realm of Your Own Personal Ignorance.* Would I want to open such a door? What was in the realm of my own personal ignorance?

Of course, I could think of nothing. Evidently, the reason for the door was to invite various personages to investigate the *"Realm of Their Own Personal Ignorance."* I was a personage! Theoretically, it was my door and I was now confronted with the door to the realm of my own personal ignorance. Did I have the courage to open it?

What might lie beyond? Would the adventure be good or bad?

I examined the door more carefully and ran my hands over the darkened wood and touched the rusted bands. I already knew all my own experiences to date. What kind of new adventure did I expect to find? I logically assumed different adventures such as travel on the high seas, or climbing Mount Everest. Then again, perhaps an intellectual adventure, like the mysteries of quantum physics, or the history of the fourteenth century, or activities in the depths of an oceanic trench. Indeed, those too would be exciting adventures, perhaps even meeting a loved one or inheriting money from a distant cousin. In other words, adventures of such variety and number they are impossible to count. Would I find all the adventures behind the door? Logically I'd have one adventure at a time; something I could reasonably absorb. I took a deep breath of courage, grabbed the handle, and swung the heavy door open wide.

> *I saw a blackened void*
> *endless in dimension*
> *where nothing will reside.*
> *From my outward looking eyes,*
> *stationary,*
> *unmoving in the darkness,*
> *I stepped,*
> *as if a tiny man,*
> *to explore the immense dark cavern.*
> *Unafraid, I went hunting*
> *through the blackness*
> *and the vastness of the void.*
> *I know there is a something,*
> *some dark secret*

somewhere lurking
on the edges of the space.

What's this?
A room of many brown faced doors,
on the walls, floor, ceiling,
each with jeweled handle thrusting,
inviting me to open.
I try the first.
A shaft of light so blinding
strikes me full upon the face.
It makes me squint,
and then the misty whiteness
of a lonely beach
and fog in wisps and clearing,
sunlight penetrating
to the rippling sand.
I see the frothy tongues
of muted waves
come licking at my toes
and biting me with cold
and in the distance,
out to sea,
I hear a joyful singing
and then the somber ringing
of a low-pitched bell,
struck in perfect measured time,
and the singing and the bell
in utter contrast mingling.
The song,
a sound of sweetness,
love and joy in living.
The bell,
a doleful measuring

of time going by.
I close the door,
reflecting,
and in a moment,
curious again,
grasp another jeweled handle.

Gently, I open
and look directly into eyes
that look directly into mine.
I see the soul of another being
as that other being searches mine.
We smile.
We cry.
We love.
We walk hand in hand
into an unlikely land
where a tree is a tree
and a me is a me.
We ask a bird, "How do you fly?"
and away on the wind he soars.
We ask the bush,
"How do you grow?"
and a flower springs from the bud.
We ask the stone,
"Why do you sit,
heavy, still,
in the heat of the desert day?"
The insect creatures beneath,
stir in the coolness,
awaiting the night.
We lie in the shade
of a pepper grove
on bluffs that fall to the sea

and watch the billowing clouds
drag their rainstorm feet.
We feel the cooler breeze
descending from the trees.
Inhale the dampened freshness
of the Eucalyptus leaves.
We hear the pattering sounds
of raindrops on our palms
and fingertips
and taste the droplets
on our lips,
so content we are to be.
A draft, ominous, cold,
from the open door and black beyond,
shatters my serenity.
I step back,
reluctantly,
through the open door,
and gently let it close.

Back again,
within the dimness of my mind,
I select another jeweled handle
and pull it once again.
I become disheartened
by a melancholy room
painted black,
yet glowing somber red,
and on a flowered platform
stands an open coffin
and a stiffened human form
lying petrified within.
I close the door
and close my eyes.

Unhappily, within my brain,
the dreadful image
I yet retain.
I look for the entrance door
and see it as before,
staring blankly in.
On the front it says,
To a Richer Life,
and as a wiser man,
I quickly open wide
and step out
to daylight,
sanity and fresh air.

I returned again to the grassy meadow on the bluff that fell steeply to the glorious sea with the afternoon sun still shining and the fair-weather clouds and salty air. I sat for a time on the grass perusing this unexpected and very personal adventure; the misty sea and softly singing voices with distant bells tolling time, a symbol of life going by. The meeting of a marvelous mate with whom I could share the joys and sorrows of my life was mine and everyone's marrlage and family. The somber coffin black room with glowing red coffin and a person lying prone within, a prediction of the end of life.

The adventure was the same as all life on this planet; the simple prediction of birth, life, and death. The greatest adventures _do_ lie within the realm of my own personal ignorance. I wake.

CONVERSATION

*(Harold is used to conversations like this. He walks
and talks among friends, searching and searching and
searching, and in the end, will he act on what was said, or
was what he said the act?)*

One o'clock.
The bulb above the table swayed
and tinked against the beaded string.
Like super rubber balls,
the nimble conversation
bounced and banged and ricocheted
across the empty cups.
One fell in my drink
and spinning, stayed.
One bruised me on the head.
Another, rolling fast, ran out the door
and down the steps to smash a bottle far away.

Charged with personality,
perfect, to the point,
the punched out P's
and tongue-tipped T's,
with points projected,
driven home,
and gesture shadows on the wall.
Conviction crammed the tongue and teeth
demanding to be freed.
Resolves were made and feelings felt,
and uppermost, the juice inside
made living more alive.

Two o'clock.
The bulb above the table, motionless, like ice.

The paralytic beaded string hanging there, precise.
The atmosphere yet pungent
with the spoken word and thought,
cleared the while the table cleared
in the stillness of the night.

What of those words,
those punchy P's and tonguey T's,
those pregnant verbal thoughts
that occupied the air?
Where are they now?
Absorbed by all the universe and gone?
Off our chest, expressed?
Into our heads to work a change
when we are down to rest?
Shall we act on what we said?
Or was what we said, the act?

PHILOSOPHY

(Harold, has reached the position of having to learn about himself and figure out where he stands on things. I have to commend him, for not to be introspective is not to have examined life, and as Socrates said, "The unexamined life is not worth living.")

My philosophy as viewed through the most sophisticated microscope is that matter, that final concrete, indivisible substance upon which I'd welcome basing my life, is absent. Each of the atoms of a rock have protons and neutrons with electrons at great relative distances, swirling about them. Is then a rock alive? And when you take the most sophisticated microscope and examine the atom, or protons and neutrons and electrons and quarks which won't stand still for experiments, as the ultimate building block for all things, they disappear into an infinity of nothingness and life that would almost seem like music.

Perhaps the big bang theory is plausible, since where there is no substance, it occupies no space, and can be crowded together into what scientists call *"the singularity."* Recent investigations have shown *"no-see-ums"* in space, a substance that's impossible to detect, and they have conveniently labeled that *"dark matter."* It seems dark matter is essential to keep galaxies from flying apart. If matter attracts matter and the stars, planets and moons of a galaxy account for only a fraction of the energy that's necessary to hold it together, what keeps the galaxies in a stable position? I really don't know. Dark matter, I guess.

My philosophy is that we are in a musical dream made up of our night sky and this planet, and though we continually discover more, we continually know less. Assuming we are in a miraculous music-like dream with galaxies, suns, planets, land, water, humans, plants and animals, and assuming we live in a miraculous terrarium, protected from the sub-freezing temperatures of minus 455 degrees Fahrenheit by a slim and deteriorating layer of gas, what then would be my philosophy?

Answer: I accept all the things my five senses tell me as true from my standpoint and that this is in the nature of human and all living species.

I accept that trees grow to fulfillment, mate, re-seed and die as do all plants, humans and animals.

I accept that a table, though a musical dream, is in fact a hard substance because that's the way it looks and feels to me.

Philosophy starts with educated life. If a living creature can't reason, there is no philosophy. Since man is the only creature, with the possible exception of dolphins and whales, that can reason, man is the only living creature that can possess a philosophy. There is faith, trust, love and the body. Love is the key ingredient to a good life. Without faith and trust there is no love, therefore an example of no good. Lack of education and love, to greater or lesser degree, I would call evil. Good, then is defined by evil, for without evil there would be no good and vice-versa. Therefore, I have faith and trust that there will be good and evil, love and no love, to a greater or lesser degree. But, without education and reason, there can be no philosophy.

I WISH TO DO IT MY WAY

But I must do it my way.
> *Can you not see the value in my way?*

I can.
> *I had another type of life for you.*

I'm sorry.
> *You are part of my dreams and expectations.*

I sense that.
> *I need you to be the way I had expected.*

I cannot.
> *My plan is perfect for you.*

I must be true to myself.
> *You'll be happier doing it my way.*

What is your way?
> *Hocus, pocus, dominocus, twenty-three skidoo.*

That's senseless.
> *Not from my standpoint.*

It is from mine.
> *Please, do it my way. For God's sake! What's the big deal?*

I'd give up my life.
> *It would be another kind of life, that's all.*

If you persist, I will become angry.
> *Don't you want my love?*

Not at that price.
> *I'll never see you again.*

Goodbye.
> *Ok! What's your way?*

Furry things. Tree life. Silly in the breeze.
> *Is it fun?*

I like it.
> *Maybe I'll try it.*

THE CHARM QUARK AND FINE LINE
(Harold investigates his greatest adventures that he knows lie within the realm of his own personal ignorance. He reads about the universe, galaxies, suns, planets, seas, land masses and elephants, but also likes to know about small things. One of the smallest is the newly named building block for all that we see, the Higgs boson. This led to the most important conjecture. He speaks!)

I was reading The God Particle, a book by Nobel Prize winner Leon Lederman, former Chief of Fermilab, the particle accelerator center in Batavia, Illinois, forty miles west of Chicago. A cyclotron particle accelerator is a four-mile underground tube with magnetic devices used for accelerating particles to nearly the speed of light, and smashing protons, neutrons, electrons, and other invisible no-see-'ems to make new elements, see what happens, and increase scientific knowledge.

It was deduced, prior to the big bang, that everything seen by the Hubble Telescope, the entire universe including earth, moon, planets, sun, stars, galaxies, and black holes was smaller than an atom before it exploded. We are a part of that explosion and, other than taking a fundamental religious position, it is difficult to perceive of geologic time, galaxy size, or more than four dimensions, but at present there's no other feasible explanation.

In one chapter, Leon was describing the parts of an atom: electron, proton, neutron. It turns out protons and neutrons are each made of six particles called quarks. They are the up, down, charm, strange, top and bottom. According to Wikipedia, quarks are fundamental particles and prime candidates for the basic building blocks of all matter. Within the dictates of the *"strong force"* called *gluons* that hold quarks together, the six rotate freely and comfortably, if not sometimes frenzied and arbitrarily, inside the proton and neutron.

In testing the power of quark-connections, Lederman injects a stream of protons, each containing six quarks, into a four-mile closed circle cyclotron all moving in one direction at close to the speed of light and bombards them with other particles moving in the opposite direction at the same speed. SMASH!!!!

They smash together! What's produced is a mess of leptons, hadrons and collateral, indescribable debris. But what of the proton? It's still intact, or maybe it splits up, or one quark goes off, bluey, or, I don't know, but what he finds out is that the family of quarks under the gluon strong force is united so powerfully it's almost impossible to break apart.

Well, that's a pretty picture, isn't it? The idea that one of the most fundamental, particles of matter, the little no-see-ums out of which everything is probably made, holds together with an impossible-to-break unity. Think of it! But, since my interests are eclectic and I accept that personalities can think freely, I took it upon myself to imagine the word *"charm"* as the catalyst meaning *"to bind irrevocably."*

HUMANS AND HOLDING TOGETHER

I was charmed by the word *"charm"* in charm quark and thought of it as a charming quark existing to show everybody how, in brand new terms, a family of six quarks linked with a strong force that cannot be broken apart is fundamental to everything that exists.

Thinking about humanity instead of science, questions arose: What is the binding force of humans that's similar to the binding force of quarks? Certainly not lying, cheating or misrepresenting. What are the constructive forces so powerful in humans they cannot be forced apart? The world is filled with opposing forces, good and evil. Good being the binding, and evil being the dividing. The binding power of quarks must be similar to the binding power of good.

Then I realized the sharp split between unification and separation, of coming together versus splitting apart and of what makes us constructive instead of destructive? There was a line that could be drawn between the binding, fundamental quark-like cohesiveness and the destructive, separating part of man. Certainly, the strength of mankind, the quark-like binding power of man, is related to the fundamental part of all connection rather than the negative. There was a line dividing the two.

A thief stealing a purse has crossed the line and operates on the destructive side of the line, therefore his act separates. The Samaritan, in returning a lost purse, operates on the constructive, quark-like side of the line and binds.

The line between constructive and destructive, unity and disunity, harmony and disharmony, sincerity and hypocrisy, and a multitude of similar opposites, I must acknowledge, has a fine dividing line.

I began to watch my own dividing line to make sure I was acting in a more quark-like, binding, impossible-to-break apart manner than otherwise.

I discovered that while walking in the neighborhood, if I waved to members of my community, they invariably waved back. I was rewarded when I took the time to wave. I acknowledged them as a friendly neighbor. My wave sent a message of security to them that I was not a threat to their existence. Their returned wave told me they acknowledged my neighborliness and returned my good message. We both won and our efforts were quark-like in that they were fundamental and binding and sent messages of contentment, mutual friendship, trust and companionship. We both were winners.

If I put my head down and avoided their eyes, if I ignored them and did not acknowledge them, what were they to think? They'd question my trustworthiness. They might ask themselves, *"Who was that guy?"* They might have made up negative, other-side-of-the-line scenarios about a questionable walker. Trust would have been broken. We both would have lost. I would not have been adding to the binding quark-like symbol I'd just discovered. To a small degree, humanity would have lost.

Listening carefully to what others say binds. Not paying attention divides. Being careful binds. Being arbitrary shows non-caring and separates. Torture does not redeem the human spirit, it separates. Of course, wars can lead to both separation and unification, so it's paramount these momentous decisions be made carefully and democratically, keeping in mind that the powerful binding of humanity is so strong that it cannot be broken apart – similar to the fundamental binding qualities of the quark family.

Reasonableness binds. Unreasonableness separates. Thinking before acting binds. Acting before thinking separates. Complementing good work binds. Non-acknowledgment of good work separates.

Doing the binding thing is not always easy. Abortion can fall on either side of the line. To make a reasonable decision requires looking inward and discovering the purpose. Purpose in the minds of different people is as dissimilar as fingerprints. What if the deciding person is not mature or educated enough to see the pitfalls? Should I be their personal educator? Should I hold a forum and get a majority of my friends to decide? The road to hell is frequently paved with good intentions. Careful consideration is the watchword. There is no simple answer.

PURPOSE

(The solution to all problems lies in purpose.)
I get into trouble if my purpose is confused. If my purpose is conflicted, a wrong decision can be made. The unsure or uneducated can turn good intentions into a bad mistake, thus crossing to the negative, separating and un-quark-like side of the line. There must be taken into account a multitude of facts and opinions.

Nevertheless, it's time I work for cohesion of all living matter, whenever I can, in both animate and inanimate considerations, and concentrate on my own side of the good line. I will then maintain a positive attitude like the quarks, the fundamental units of all matter, held together by the strong force, so intent on binding and cohesiveness, they cannot be broken apart.

A simple digression. There are two things I've accepted, but don't ever expect to know.

(1) How did the big bang come about, especially if it began tinier than an atom and then exploded into such a huge and complex vision as the whole universe?

(2) On our four-and-a-half-billion-year-old planet, what motivated the first gene to stay alive and fight against all other competing genes for life?

A few opposites:

binding	*as against*	*separating*
hospitable	*as against*	*inhospitable*
welcoming	*as against*	*unwelcoming*
tasteful	*as against*	*distasteful*
friendly	*as against*	*unfriendly*
sincerity	*as against*	*insincerity*
warmth	*as against*	*coldness*

(The process of decaying protons is called the "weak force", though I don't see how decomposition can be

called a force, but that's not the issue here.)

I was charmed by the charm quark which is a second-generation quark with a charge of +2/3 and is the third most massive of quarks at about 1-1/2 times the size of a proton. I don't know what this means, but I know it's very important. They tried to separate them with the Fermilab cyclotron and it was revealed that the more powerful the separation attempt, the more powerfully the quarks united. Shouldn't it be so with humanity?

THE SEARCH

(Learning to be introspective, Hal thinks about the past. He's learned that he may need help in his quest, even though he's not sure what he's questing. Let's go along with him.)

Hello, Doctor.
> *Hello, what can I do for you?*

I have a question.
> *Ask, please.*

How can I protect myself from knowing my intrinsic worthiness?
> *A good question, my son.*

Can you shed some light, Doctor, on how I'm to protect myself?
> *Why do you ask?*

I don't know if I should love myself or not.
> *Who is yourself?*

I don't know. That's why I'm here.
> *How can I help you decide whether you love yourself if you can't tell me who yourself is?*

I thought there might be some other way.
> *Well, you could develop a neurosis.*

I already have one.
> *How does it affect you?*

Insomnia, nervousness, high blood pressure, indigestion.
> *I'm so sorry.*

Just what is a neurosis, Doctor?
> *The basis of neurosis is ignorance or lies you tell yourself to protect you from knowing the truth of your worthiness.*

My neurosis doesn't seem to be doing the job.
> *You could develop a new symptom that might take your mind off having to learn who you are so you*

could decide if you are love-worthy or not.
I'm practically dead from the four symptoms I have,
Doctor. I would prefer not to have to add another one.
> *Why don't you look into who you are? Maybe you will be pleasantly surprised or at least be OK in your own eyes.*

The risk is too great.
> *You mean, down deep, you suspect there's a 70-30 chance you're not worthy of your own affection?*

Yep! That's it! The risk is too great!
> *Have you ever thought of becoming obsessed with Jesus or joining a Hare-Krishna group or some kind of cult where some authority figure would absolve you of all your supposed or real sins and would love you even if, in your own eyes, you were still not worthy?*

I'm not the religious type.
> *How about other forms of self-destruction? How about doing dangerous stunts for TV? If you don't get killed, you could make lots of money. You could blow things up ....*

No! No! No! I just want to feel good and live out my life in a normal constructive manner. Perhaps even contribute to world harmony or something.
> *How about suicide? There are new painless ways ...*

Sometimes I feel like it. I usually don't feel <u>that</u> bad. Just moderately punky.
> *You know, Sol, I care about you.*

You do?
> *Of course I do.*

You got any degrees or anything?
> *I'm a Doctor. I have taken special training in my field. I'm competent. It says so right on my license. Why do you ask about degrees?*

What does it mean to me if a moderately competent

Doctor cares about me?

You mean if I had more degrees; if I was really some-
body, like a Pope or a president and cared about you,
then you would feel better about yourself and your
neurotic symptoms would go away and you would
begin to live a life of self-fulfillment and joy?

Sounds kind of ridiculous, when you put it that way,
Doctor.

I think you needed your mother and father to love
you.

I wished mother had loved me.

Didn't your mother love you?

She said she did.

Didn't you believe her?

I guess I did.

Why are you being vague?

It's just the _way_ she said it.

You mean if she told you she loved you in just the
right way, you might have believed her?

Am I being too picayune?

I don't think so. Where is your mother now?

Des Moines.

Why don't you call her?

I called her last week. She's into her life and doesn't seem
to care what I do anymore.

You still hope to get her to tell you she loves you in just
the right way?

She never changes.

How long have you been trying to get her to say she
loves you in just the right way?

For years now.

All your life?

All my life.

Sounds like you haven't changed either.

That's different.

What do you mean, different?

Mothers are supposed to love you in just the way you need them to love you.

Is that written down somewhere?

Are you trying to trap me? You're just trying to trap me! If you continue to pursue this line with me, I shall have to cancel our appointment!

Do so, if you feel the need.

Well, watch it!

Sorry.

You don't care!

Yes, I do.

No you don't.

Yes, I do.

Yeah? How much?

A lot!

You liar! You don't know me that well. I just came in here today. I've known you for about a half-hour and already you say you care about me. You lie!

I care about the human species.

Oh? Now I'm not human?

Of course you're human. I care about you even though I've only known you for about a half-hour.

Yeah? How much?

We've been through that.

But you've never answered it to my satisfaction.

I love you one hundred percent.

You do?

Yes, I do.

I still don't feel good.

Don't you think it's about time you faced the real issues? Why don't you do some introspection, find out who you really are so you can decide if you are

worthy of your own love?
OK. I guess I'll try.
Thank you.
How do I do that?

MINDFULNESS
(Do we need to know a fine line between mindfulness and mindlessness? Apparently, Harold does.)

Imagine a young guy, let's call him Bill, walking across the street thinking of his girlfriend, of which he just had a terrific lunch time with her in her apartment. Let's say he's going back to work in downtown New York. It's very crowded with people going this way and that, sometimes swerving to miss one another, most walking briskly to all the places of which I couldn't conceive in a dog's age, and this one guy finds himself following the crowd across the busy street, deep in thought about how good he feels and the miraculous wonders of the sleeping female he just left.

Suddenly a truck blasts its horn as it swerves, barely missing him, and the driver yells an obscenity before he's further affronted by a the truck driver's obscene gesture as he trips on the curb. Very embarrassing! Very unmindful! The stoplight had changed and Bill wasn't being mindful! He was extremely mindful about his lunch period, but not mindful about crossing the street. We can all do better than that, can't we? Yes! Be mindful when crossing the street!

Of course, it's good to be mindful about everything in the whole world at all times, but that's a very big task. Even little things are important; like walking along a dirt pathway in the mountains of a National Park. One must keep an eye on the path to avoid stepping on a stone and twisting an ankle, especially when it's far from an Urgent Care Hospital. Watch your step high in the mountains of National Parks, OK? Be mindful!

Also, while driving, be aware of any oncoming truck and don't, while leaning down to find a life saver under the seat, accidentally cross the double yellow line or you might be surprised to find yourself in the Emergency Ward with a bandage over one eye and a leg hanging in the air. Finding things under the car seat while driving, crossing yellow lines, and hitting trucks is being unmindful!

Then, there are all kinds of dark holes; ones in the garage behind a pile of boxes, or a dusty chair waiting for over a year to be fixed, or holes in a messy closet behind sweaters and shoes, or ones in the park under a rock that look like tiny caves. Don't put your hand in a dark hole that looks like a tiny cave. You don't know what's in there. That's not living mindfully. There might be a poisonous snake in there or a mad porcupine or a funny spider with an hourglass figure. It might be good to get down on your knees with your face close to the hole and peer into the blackness, but if a skunk's in there, he might spray your eyes - then where would you be? You could shove a stick in there, but you might make whatever's in there angry, like a bobcat or raccoon, who'd snarl out in a raging fury and bite your nose. If you carried one with you, you might throw a bomb in there for safety's sake, but then you'd destroy the entire hole and whatever's in there, like a mother rabbit with her babies cowering in fear, but now are only bits of paws and heads flying through the air. You wouldn't want to hurt a bunch of bunnies, would you? Or, God forbid, if some grossly little ugly alien creature crawled out with eight tentacles wiggling, and a thousand little pinhole eyes with a hole in the top of its head, making alarmed little grunts and smelling like something dead from the Pleistocene age appeared, you'd raise your hand to your mouth, cry out, and shrink back in horror. Probably not, but with black holes, you'd never know. Don't stick your hand in black holes. OK?

On the other hand, I have to admit, I did something unmindful just yesterday. I try to watch myself, but I'm not perfect and that's all right. It's OK! I own it. Usually, when I go to bed, I put a book and glasses on the shelf behind my head. The theory is that I would read a page or two before going to sleep while waiting for Marge to come to bed. Well, I got my book on the shelf all right, and then went to brush my teeth, but Marge came to bed right away and she was sleepy and so was I, so I turned out the light without reading and we went to sleep. The next morning I went to put my book away and did I find my glasses on top of the book? No! I found my toothbrush. A book and toothbrush on a cabinet on the back of the bed! What's that all about?

Live life mindfully and take every action throughout the day and night in full awareness of simple things, from tying shoelaces to tip-toeing along the narrow top of a windy, 70 stories high I-beam with an aerial view of the roofs and pavement below, with tiny cars and buses moving like ants quietly along. It's the only way! LIVE MINDFULLY!

NOT POLITE

(Thinking about mankind's brief period of three-million years on the face of this miraculous earth and doing wishful thinking about some kind of life after death, Harold would like to live a healthy and passionate life on this earth longer than his 84 years.)

At the speed of light
times ten,
the star moves away from me.
Where is it going?
Why so fast?
Why does it go at all?
It should be content
to remain in place
and behave,
that I may study it,
take notes,
exhaust it's secrets.
I'm not used to
things retreating,
things so big,
things so bright,
things ferocious in the night.
A star should stick around,
keep me company,
advise me when I'm sick,
entertain me when I'm well.
I should take a star for granted,
but it won't let me.
Insists on blazing away
at the speed of light,
times ten,
burning with the audacity

of a million suns,
going to places I'd never go.
Rocketing away
through a frozen night,
not looking back,
not thinking of me,

NOT POLITE!

SPIRITS

(Harold has a few questions: do spirits have sex in the afterlife? As he's heard reports claim, sex after death would require a body of some substance, weight, and form. It's said the body dies but the spirit remains. Yes, he knows it remains with those still living, but also another spirit of the dead goes somewhere beyond without the substance of its former body. If a former living creature has no body, it has no senses and therefore can't experience anything. If it doesn't have a body, it can't have sex, certainly in the same manner as when alive.)

Do spirits have feelings? I don't know! But if they do, they certainly do _not_ have a body with which to sense them and so if they do, they wouldn't feel them the way I would if I were alive.

Can I have a personal relationship on the other side? Can a *"passed on spirit"* fall in love with another *"passed on spirit?"* Can one spirit harbor a dislike for another spirit? If love and hate are possible in the other place, then spirits must have feelings. But with no body, what feels the feelings?

Is there grossness and decorum on the other side? Is there the *"right thing to do"* and the *"wrong thing to do?"* If so, who judges? Who sets the rules? Are there rules on the other side?

If there are right and wrong, love and hate, grossness and decorum with rules such as the Golden Rule *(do unto others as you would have them do unto you)*, the BRIEF YEARS OF LIFE, then ETERNAL LIFE AFTER DEATH is not too different than my experience during my own brief life. Is life after death the same as life before death? Where were we before we were born? Seems we're missing thirteen billion years of eternity.

Is there food after death? Is there lemon meringue pie? Coffee? Donuts? Obviously not, since a spirit has no body, no digestive system, no taste buds. Perhaps, one might say, *"Yes, the living after dying can enjoy all those things in a way in which I as a mere mortal cannot conceive. They may enjoy other things, even more glorious than pie, donuts, coffee, or sex. Enjoy them in such a way a mortal can never know."*

I cannot know what a butterfly feels when it mates. Nor can I know, like the Great White Shark, what it's like to sense faint electrical charges moving through the water from many miles away. Nor can I know what life is like for the worm buried in its comfortable home deep in the ground.

If I find it impossible to understand what a spirit's life is like, I also find it impossible to understand what our fellow living creatures life is like. I couldn't say what a spirit's life is like any more than I could tell you what a hummingbird feels drinking nectar from a morning glory or during sex, or answer the question of how a homing pigeon finds its way home from a thousand miles away.

It's impossible to describe the inner experience of some of our own living creatures. Who can tell me what its like to have the inner life of a lion or a python or jungle frog or a killer bee or a termite or an iguana or an elephant or a snow leopard or an octopus or an eagle or a starfish or a sea cucumber or a grub worm or a penguin or a seal or an amoeba or a tree or an orchid or dandelion or potato or a green blade of grass?

If you can find me A BEING who knows what its like to be inside any of the forgoing, you will also find me A BEING who might have a ghost of a chance of telling me what its like to be a spirit on the other side of death.

As I observe, everyone has THE WILL TO LIVE. The

thought of <u>*NOT*</u> living is devastating to most of us! *(I envision an eternal, coma-like unconsciousness.)* As I see it, apparently the hereafter will take care of itself. Given good health and a good life, lets face it, we all wish we wouldn't die.

COSMIC CLOCK

In a single tick
of the Cosmic Clock,
I'm strata.
I walk through space
and step through faith.
I am a process
always in motion,
my grave my destination.

I AM

I am.
I hear.
I see.
I feel.
I have energy.
I have latent energy.
My energy waits.
I reign it in.
I do not release it.
I am filled with it
to the brim.
I save it.
My heart beats quietly,
solemnly,
waiting,
powerfully,
capable of delivering
all the I am there is,
soon!

IN BETWEEN

(Since Hal knew many of the 50's songs and loved to sing in the shower or car, and has a somewhat out-of-tune voice with limited range, he jokingly told his kids they could either have a CD recording of <u>Father Harold Sings</u> or a CD recording of <u>Beethoven's Fifth played at 45 speed</u>. They never laughed, but this broke him up. He's not clear how they took it, but selecting either is less than a perfect solution. The fine line of selection arose between the two negatives: father's bad recording of himself, or Beethoven's Fifth played much too slow.)

The CD scenarios are like being caught *"between a rock and a hard place."* Either alternative is disastrous. Consider an easy one: I'm going to cross the street, but a car is coming, so I decide to wait until the car passes, then I'll cross the street. Not too complex, right?

Consider a harder one: there's heavy traffic at a busy intersection; I'm in a hurry, but the light is against me. I can decide to: *(1)* break the law by jaywalking, or *(2)* go to the corner and wait for the light, then cross.

Being in a hurry, heavy traffic, and going against the light are added complexities that complicate the choice. Consequences must always be paid, and getting there on time and the possibility of being hit by a car are all critically related. The fine line of decision, the IN BETWEEN of resolution, is now based on multiple decisions that need to be made simultaneously. And that brings up questions such as: Am I a risk taker, or do I play it safe? Am I thoughtless or mindful, or an average of the two? What would a thoughtful, mindful guy do?

But then, it is within my character to make simple problems a full scale dilemma. I believe things are never either all one way or all the other. Perhaps I could play it like this: I'm in a hurry, but it's not life or death. There's heavy traffic, but I'm well-coordinated and can dart between the cars. I'm mindful and won't move until I'm sure I can go!

But then I have to make an even bigger problem out of a simple decision. I'm IN BETWEEN because, whether I like it or not, it involves the fine line between opposites, and now it has to do with which part of me does the deciding; my left brain or my right brain. I know that cars, trees, pavement, animals, birds, fish, mountains, ocean, air, clouds, stones, plants and trees, and giraffes really have no choice. They're stone-cold dead to reasoning, being governed only by instinct.

Living creatures other than humans, in proportion to their size, don't have as large a brain as humans. Instinct drives animals! See danger - run! See food - eat! Find mate - procreate! It's also true that people have two sides to their brains, connected by a thin membrane called the corpus callosum. Each side of the brain operates differently, with one side usually dominant over the other. Do I cross the street by INSTINCT, or do I cross the street with REASON?

Tests show the right brain is instinctual and manages emotions, music, color, images, intuition and creativity, and the left-brain manages reason, language, logic, critical thinking and numbers. Considering I'm indecisive and IN BETWEEN in my thinking, this all involves HOW I cross the street.

When decisions are tough, the reasoning portion of the human brain is the best portion of the brain to resolve the dilemma. Dinosaurs dominated the planet for 135-million years and they did so without a reasoning left side of the brain. On the subject of instinct and being much in the category of the Acid Sea of Reality, I'm reminded of a funny/tragic little story I wrote about Hummer, the bunny, and Spanker, the shepherd dog.

Hummer, a vegetarian little bunny, grew fat and happy eating grandma's carrots. Spanker saw him one day, pounced on him, and ate him on the spot. Later, Spanker went home where he was fed and fell asleep by the fire. That was the final end of the Hummer-Spanker story. Both Hummer and Spanker had integrity.

Hummer was true to his bunnyness and the sheppard was true to his doggyness. There was no fine line between opposites, no IN-BETWEEN, or indecision. They had no reasoning part of their brain with which to confuse themselves. This automatically meant they fell into the category of animals brought about by the great forces of nature and governed totally by instinct. Nevertheless, they each possessed that miraculous, dependable quality humans love so much called *integrity*.

Let's forget my condition of being IN BETWEEN when crossing the street question, and say I want an ice cream cone. This follows from the impulses of the instinctual right brain. It's sweet! It's chocolaty, it's cold, I'm hot and sweaty, it feels good in my mouth and it makes me feel full. I want one! My right brain says, *"yeah!"*

But, the left brain kicks in. I'm a little overweight. I promised myself I'd go light on sweets but I'm proud I haven't had sweets for a couple of weeks. Perhaps I deserve a little break. Sometimes one can be too hard on one's self. Nobody who'd criticize me will know. I'll get one!

Or perhaps there's another end to the story: I won't get one! And here we have the simplest example of IN BETWEEN or the fine line between opposites. Should I yield to the more primitive, emotional, intuitive right brain, or should I continue in good health and listen to my relatively new, logical, analytical, reasoning left brain?

Animals have no choice. Fish have no choice. Trees and

bushes have no choice. Water, earth, clouds, sky, the moon, the sun have no choice. I don't know about elephants, whales and porpoises, but as far as I know, *only humans are blessed and cursed with the miracle of the left brain and choice.* Perhaps that's what the bible meant when it said that of all the creatures, humans shall be given a CHOICE to eat or not eat the apple.

In life, love it or hate it, we are stuck with our instincts! I for one can't survive without them. I love my instincts. And yet, if we have the LEFT BRAIN to countermand, we can decide to retract all or portions of our instincts! In some ways, being given the miracle of choice is a cruel joke. In tough areas we're forced into conflict: we're IN BETWEEN. We desperately want an ice cream cone, but we don't at the same time. We have a CHOICE of selecting what's good or bad for us.

Forgetting things as simple as ice cream cones, the activities of the left brain hold out the *only* hope for mankind on this planet. Do I have faith mankind will take the next evolutionary step and allow the reasoning portion of their brains to dominate? Given the history of humans since the Stone Age, and being a percentage man about predicting the future, I see little hope for present mankind to evolve so quickly. I know the reasoning left brain is the only hope for keeping the planet a personal heaven. It's my thought that only the left brain can make the reasonable decisions to stop relentless overpopulation, correct global warming, eliminate nuclear bombs, stop wars, institute global education, cultivate trees, clean our oceans and stop treating the earth as if it's our own private garbage dump. And I might add, halt the terrifying future of drones, fracking, hacking of Internet systems, and blasting the oceans with sounds that destroy the hearing of our archetypal neighbors, whales and dolphins, and unify all religious and political organizations.

Only the left brain can institute justice and fair play and make judicious use of our raw materials, improve our planet and create peace between all people, etc. Yes, an impossible order! The left brain was not created to justify the improper, destructive impulses of the more primitively-oriented right brain. Perhaps life is in the FATE category, but I, as a human, pray that humans can quickly evolve and this IN BETWEEN dilemma be solved.

DREAM

(Harold tries to match his stars. Perhaps his book will help him think things out. He thinks he's almost got it, but in the study, the stars don't quite match. Perhaps he needs more education, more knowledge, more discoveries in that vast realm of his so-called ignorance.)

I am outside.
It is twilight.
I take points of light,
like diamonds,
and arrange them on the ground.
Two stars (points) are larger
and have special power,
and so I arrange them
in such a position
it will strengthen the lower "cross"
of the design,
so that when I pick it up,
it will not fall apart.
When I have the diamonds,
or points, properly arranged,
and the real stars have come out.
I grasp the design,
(it has edges that are graspable)
and hold it up to the sky.
I try to match my design
with real stars.
I try to get my diamond design
to fall in exact sync
with the real stars.
I'm compelled to get them
to match up.
When they do,

something wonderful will happen.
Two neighbors come out
from nearby homes
and watch me do this.
They think I'm a strange,
poetic, philosophic,
sort of fellow.
I sense they approve of me,
and think of me as somehow, special.
I feel their warmth and respect,
even though I suspect
their skepticism and humor
toward me.
Yet, it is important I match my stars
with the real stars, and I continue,
though my arms are tired
from holding them up.
I cannot get more than one or two stars
to match my design.

REALITY

("Make reality your friend" was a phrase often coined by Marge. It had been recurring to him lately in regard to another phrase meaning the opposite, "Live in Fantasy." According to Marge, if he does not face reality, he is forced to live in fantasy.)

Fantasy seems to be an idea more acceptable to some than others. I'll give you an example.

I thought to myself, I know I'll pass that test even though I've not studied. Well, of course, I took the test and flunked. Why? Because I didn't study. I didn't face reality, which were the facts. I didn't move the boat because my oars weren't in the water. Why? I was tired of the subject. I didn't need that course to graduate, anyway. I was out last night drinking and too bombed to worry about it. I didn't like my parents forcing me to study a hateful course and this was my passive-aggressive method of revolt. There can be a million reasons why I took the path of flunking, not all of which may be known in my conscious mind.

What if I didn't pass the course because my unconscious mind wouldn't allow it? *(That's a reason the left brain might justify the wishy-washiness of the right brain. Of course, the unconscious mind might be working for the organism's best. I'm sure I'll never know.)*

There are infinite reasons why I may not live in reality. *(I have to ask myself at this time: Whose reality? My mother's? My own? My dad's reality? Societies?)*

Nevertheless, digression excused, to live in reality is to – GULP! – face the facts!

I try! I try! But there are so many reasons why I can't. There could be old, unconscious issues stored away in my unexamined mind forcing me not to study, or just an ineffective conscious mind, lazy excuses, or not being smart. Yes! Ignorance could be my problem. I may be too dumb to face reality or too angry to face reality.

I might visualize a conversation with myself, *"Heck! I thought I was doing OK and now I'm bummed! They tell me I'm not facing reality."* It seems simplistic to ask why I, or any person, might live inside a fantasy world while reality is so blatantly ever-present. Except, to me, reality isn't so blatantly ever-present.

From a world standpoint, at any given second reality exists! At this tiny, infinitesimal moment in time, a war is raging, wounded soldiers are suffering or recuperating, icebergs are slipping into the sea, the world population alarmingly continues to rise and America moves deeper into debt. North Korea is developing nuclear bombs, fifty percent of the world's population suffers from malnutrition, and only one percent, so the latest study goes, has a working computer to help them think, etc. This is the present world reality and all the wishing, thinking, hoping and praying cannot make the slightest change. Reality is what it is. *REALITY IS WHAT IS!*
WHAT DOES THAT MEAN?

NOW YOU SEE IT, NOW YOU DON'T
(Harold is imagining a blown-up planet?
Can we forgive him?)

Little particles of teeth,
Lashes and legs
Skittering through the void
And particles of peach pits
And panty hose
Plunging
Between the stars.
Salt water droplets
A fin
A scale
And fish eye or two
Making an interstellar beeline
And tear drop shapes
Of frozen tooth paste
(They glowed
They gleamed
They glummed)
Toward Jupiter
And beyond
Flashes
Of broken bottle bits
A rock
A tree
Some arid extra-dry,
And me
Pierce the universal night
On a cosmogonic flight
But no one to see.

LIFE IN PROCESS AND CONTEXT
(Must we really discuss life in its process and context?)

Life, as all that lives, exists in process and context. As humans, we control what we can, then deal with fate. Given complete control, let's say as a talented architect with a rich, cooperative client, the architect can achieve almost total harmony. There is a rule for the achievement of harmony: *Every element shall be designed within the context of the next larger element.*

Architecturally speaking, there is a strong relationship between any new design and the context within which it will exist. The new design and its context in which it will exist will have to like each other. That means the controlling force, the architect or designer, must have compassion and caring for both.

For example, were I to design an accessory, let's say a flower bowl or salt and pepper shakers or select a painting for a wall, I would make sure it was within the context of the space and furnishings. If I were to select or design furnishings, they should be selected or designed within the context of the next larger element, the house. If I were to design a house, I must be considering the next larger element, the property. Were I designing the property, I must take into consideration the neighborhood. If neighborhood, then community, if community, then surrounding terrain, etc., to the end of the universe.

However, without being an architect with a rich cooperative client, but just living as an ordinary person, everything is in some kind of processing and context, good or bad, anyway. Though we may be free to design ourselves, it is usually under conditions not of our making. *Fate* or conditions not of our making affect us negatively or positively, but usually both, and to a greater or lesser degree, affect our actions, dictate our moods, change our way of thinking, make us angry or happy and create joy or despair. Our emotional and mental life is influenced, greatly or moderately or minimally, by the context in which we live.

While battling my own demons from 1966-1968, while the economy was in the doldrums, and while we had just moved into our new house with mortgage and property taxes at their highest, my life was bombarded by the normal variety of world happenings. For me, they affected me negatively, moderately and positively.

Normal tensions then were exacerbated by the knowledge that the United States and Russia were in a cold war and each had weapons capable of annihilating all living things. *(Affected me negatively.)*

Frequent reports of the daily Vietnam War body count and what kind of world were we making for our children? *(Affected me negatively.)*

Peripheral awareness that 400,000 people would perish over the next three years in China during the *"great proletariat cultural revolution."* Chairman Mao Zedong, his wife, Jiang Qing, and their Red Guards irreparably damaged monasteries, manuscripts and priceless works of art and caused havoc within China's intellectual community. In a paranoia about the spread of Capitalism, China created a cultural disaster in its own country. *(Affected me negatively.)*

Egypt, Syria and Jordan were attacked by Israel who, in the Arab-Israeli six-day war, occupied the Gaza strip, the Sinai Peninsula and Golan Heights. *(Affected me moderately.)*

Grissom, White and Chaffee were burned in the capsule of the Saturn 1-B rocket while still on the ground. *(Affected me negatively.)*

Huey Newton became leader of the Black Panthers who wanted power, full employment, land, bread, housing, education, clothing and justice. Political power *"comes through the barrel of a gun"* was one of the Black Panthers' doctrines. Armed recruits with dark glasses patrolled ghettos to protect residents. A raised arm with a fist was a symbol that struck fear into most whites' hearts. When Eldridge Cleaver superseded Huey Newton's leadership, the group advocated overthrow of the government; that attracted the FBI, who attacked them and forcibly dismantled their organization. *(Affected me moderately.)*

The Arno River near Florence Italy overflowed and flooded great parts of the city, ruining artistic masterworks; many beyond repair, leaving others to be laboriously restored. *(Affected me moderately.)*

Thurgood Marshall became the first black man to sit on the Supreme Court, bringing a new perspective to the Civil Rights movement. *(Affected me positively.)*

Peggy Fleming won a gold medal in figure skating in the Olympics. Jim Ryun ran a mile in three minutes, fifty-one and three-tenths seconds. Truman Capote published *In Cold Blood*. Dustin Hoffman starred in *The Graduate*. The Beatles released *Sergeant Pepper's Lonely Hearts Club Band*. *(Affected me positively.)*

While I was in process with my home and business life, all this information affected me positively, moderately or negatively. Within the times of my living I was also in process and context. The context of the world affected me probably less than the process and context of my home life and business life, but nevertheless I, as well as everyone living with me, was affected by it. Our lives were lived in PROCESS while in CONTEXT.

THE THOUGHT

(Hal wrote this poetic attempt to visualize how it would feel if he had already attained some powerful epiphany. Things had gone awry for him recently and he was desperate to find out what he'd been missing. The hoped for The Thought, if it came at all, would change his life, irrevocably, for the better. After 50 years of living, he thought The Thought was about to emerge. In desperation, he hoped, he prayed.)

The thought
strikes me full
like some silver ray
from a mighty star.

It pierces my mind
and bursts,
flooding the interior
with bright, white light.
I have a new perspective.

The thought,
comes swinging through
like some mighty ax
with gleaming blade.

It strikes the trunk
and fells the tree,
and I know that my lost ...
is well fed,
ready for caring and love.

From my entrails,
the thought

wells up
and becomes one
with mind, body, and spirit.

It sits, shining on my shoulder
like Lili's silver bird
and sings (golden trumpets)
musical truths,
glorious, in my ear.

The thought,
when I relax,
pours out golden,
honey-rays,
brimming, spilling,
letting me know
that I am ...,
and certainty
sits within me,
a strong foundation
for action.

The thought
I work.
I wait.

ARIANA

(Harold buys a piece of art! And sorrows and joys in the past provide sorrows and joys in the present due to a would-be-simple purchase. Everyone would face similar sorrows and joys because everyone at one time or another must stare down The Acid Sea of Reality.)

In our many years of Sunday trips to visit Ojai art galleries, Marge and I had admired a 22-inch female nude sculpture with flame-like hair gesticulating like a wild, dancing goddess. Considering its perfectionist quality, the price was not exorbitant, and over years of visiting the gallery we were always surprised it had not been sold. While walking Ojai's covered sidewalks, and on what seemed like a whim, but may have been a preordination, I said under my breath, *"I'd like to own that sculpture."*

I expected Marge's answer to be something like, *"Yes, wouldn't it be nice."* And we'd continue our day. But I was surprised when she said, *"Why not give yourself something for a change? You've worked hard all your life."*

Then I surprised myself when I gave serious thought to the ownership of that fine sculpture. We returned to have another look. But after listening to salesperson Maureen's reasons why we loved and deserved it, I continued to be embarrassed and shy at thoughts of ownership and we left, assuring Maureen we'd sleep on it and give her our decision the next day.

On the long drive home we discussed having it in our home, and I told Marge the sculpture would be such a powerful presence in our household we'd be forced to re-evaluate our lives every time she came into view. And though I felt slightly intimidated by her, we chose a name, *"Riana,"* and, undecided, slept on it that night.

The next day, I woke up with the name _Ariana_. Marge

and I agreed that name was a better one and I called Maureen to tell her I was sending her a letter and check to put Ariana on layaway. I wanted to tell her what Ariana meant to us and why it was important for the sculpture to be with us. In effect, the letter said,

"I thought George's (George La Fayette's) figure was one of passion, intelligence and openness. One who directly embraces reality and the qualities I'd like to see in myself.

Marge enjoyed the figure as being in the world, working with facts, as they exist, rather than trying to deal with an always-unproductive fantasy. She enjoys the figure as an open, powerful, wild lady she recognizes as part of herself; a young woman who deals with the world on the world's terms.

Marge, a mother, therapist, artist, and dancer, likes that the figure invites us to move our bodies. There's an unashamed aliveness about her and though sculptors like Maillot can make figures bursting with life, his sculptures are more reflective and introspective than the wild lady. They don't enjoy the attitude of attack on what needs to be done with Ariana's relish.

If Marge sees Ariana as part of herself, I see her as someone I'm privileged to love. We welcome her into our family. Thank you, Maureen, for understanding the beauty of this artwork and realizing that for it, Marge and I were perfect."

Two Sundays later we returned to Ojai, paid Maureen, and drove the sculpture home. Maureen had spoken to the artist, George La Fayette, and read him my letter. He was pleased with my comments and told Maureen his work was called *The Fire Dancer*.

Fire Dancer! We owned *The Fire Dancer*! She sat on the cabinet next to the dining room table where she could be clearly seen three times a day. In the evening she remained every bit a presence as I'd predicted and dramatically claimed her space. She was graceful. She was wild. Her gesture, like that of a deity, was a goddess that demanded attention. I don't think I'm superstitious, but when I learned she was called *The Fire Dancer*, I thought I knew why I'd felt intimidated. Fire is a bad omen for me. Our possession of *The Fire Dancer* might predict another ordeal by fire.

Many years ago, in my other marriage, we watched our dream house burn to the ground. It was caught in a Malibu brush fire along with many other houses including the celebrated Serra Retreat. Towering in flame before collapsing on itself, our house took another week of smoking and agonizing before finally settling into a slim pile of gray ashes overlain with crossing strips of black, melted steel I-beams. My three grown daughters, two of whom have children of their own, are still frightened of California fires and our family still becomes agitated in too-hot weather and strong offshore winds. I did not want to feel intimidated by *The Fire Dancer* and in the evening tried to rationalize it away before finally drifting off to sleep.

I dreamt Ariana was administering charms to a smoldering island between Java and Sumatra called Krakatoa. In 1883, the island was blown into non-existence by a volcano so strong its sound was heard in India and Australia. It caused an immense tsunami, killing 40,000 people and sending waves as far away as France. For a hundred years the island kept building above and sinking below the surface of the Indian Ocean, but now in the dream Ariana darkly hovers over this mountainous shape, still steaming, nervous and uncommitted.

The dream slipped silently into another; two islands that metamorphosed into rocky moons, Phobos and

Deimos, revolving around Mars and a myth about the God of War who assumed himself betrayed and sent wayward lovers to hell by turning them into immense boulders and hurtling them forever around his fiery planet. Their fate was immutable, endlessly chasing each other, overtaking and passing with fleeting glances, but never meeting, always heartbroken and perpetually cold. Was it Ariana that provoked these dreams?

Upon awakening the word *"intimidation"* leaped into my mind. Fire intimidated me. Ariana was *The Fire Dancer,* so Ariana intimidated me. *She* was a bad omen! *The Fire Dancer was* a symbol of the fires of hell? If she were actually the God of Fire, I could be in for some disastrous, fiery event which was the source of the intimidation.

I wanted to like Ariana. As the recipient of reason, I reasoned I could avail myself of the gift! *Fire Dancers* like fire. Fire was the mother of *The Fire Dancer.* But then it occurred to me that *The Fire Dancer,* like fire, brightness and heat, was like the fiery sun. The sun and fire were interdependent! The sun is fire! Without the sun consuming itself by fire and the earth being at the proper distance from the sun, there would be no life. She's not the *Snow Dancer* or *God of the Frigid North.* If she liked cold she'd be dressed warmly, but she's naked, therefore she's already warm; perhaps even hot! She's a hot lady! The earth magically spins through the black vacuum of space at minus 270 degrees Celsius. Yet the planet is close enough to the sun to receive just the right amount of light and heat to sustain luxuriant life. Our ancestor's first discovery was fire and they used it to keep warm and cook food. Today fire is priceless. Therefore, fire is good. What better than to own a *The Fire Dancer* who likes fire, heat, light, energy, and so much the better if she's actually the God of Fire? I discovered Ariana likes the same things I like. This thought brought me a sigh of relief. She's not just the symbol of uncontrolled fire, but also of *controlled* fire.

After my run and shower, I looked at her again and thought, though well-named by the artist, she really didn't have to be *The Fire Dancer*. She has no nameplate. I don't have to call her *The Fire Dancer*. Without a name she still has the same female power. In the morning sun, on the cabinet, casting spells out the window over all of nature, her naked presence is just as strong whether or not *The Fire Dancer* is her name. I looked deeply into her eyes for I've learned, in humans they reveal the person's true nature. I did so and expected her eyes to look straight ahead matching her body's direct bearing, but no, her eyes looked mysteriously to one side. I wondered at the artist making those tiny elliptical eyes with a diameter of less than a sixteenth of an inch. I marveled at George's focus of attention and steady hand that could fashion something so delicate and full of meaning. The expression is that of a mysteriously alive deity contemplating an enigmatic enterprise that only exists in her present form. The gesture of her physical presence is neither caring nor uncaring. She is neither for me nor against me. She is OF me. In fact, she is OF THE UNIVERSE and that reminds me of the Big Bang, the expanding cosmos, our planet, and everything on it. We're all the same; galaxy, sun, planets, rocks, water and living things, neither for nor against, neither good nor evil, and the water-glass, as each of us chooses, is either half-full or half-empty. We, Ariana, and all that is known are a magnificent IS!

Ariana no longer intimidates me, she inspires me, and I see her now as the UNIVERSAL FORCE. We need George La Fayette, for without him I wouldn't have my final philosophy so vividly expressed in the soul, spirit, and three dimensions of Ariana.

YOU GOT ME THINKING

If reality is your friend,
not to pursue it
is to opt for fantasy,
which results in knowing less,
and being less aware,
which is a move toward
unconsciousness,
and ultimately, death.

To pursue reality
is to opt for knowing,
which is to become more aware,
which is a move toward
higher consciousness,
and a richer life experience.

Some opt for fantasy
out of fear of knowing,
which means they are
protective
of that which they don't wish to know.
To move from Fear-protection to Love-learning
requires moving through pain issues,
yet expressed in rich learning.

SOUL

(Hal was thinking about his soul the other day. He didn't know why. He guessed he'd used the word so often at times without thinking he'd never got into what the word really means.)

Of course, people like reverends, pastors, or ministers, or those belonging to organized religions, use the word soul all the time, assuming, I guess, others know what they're talking about. The first definition in Wikipedia says soul is *the incorporeal essence of a person or living thing*. Well, I guess The Wik's got it right, and now I need to figure out what IS the incorporeal essence of myself. At least I already know I'm living, so that part of the definition is solved.

Wik also says that in some religions it is God that creates a person's soul. Well, Duh! I guess, I sure as heck know he does! But then I ask myself which God he's talking about. In that argument, the world never seems to agree. If many people have different conclusions about what God is, and I am one of the many people, then I should be allowed a comment, too. Yes! I know I'm no better than anybody else, but then, probably no worse.

To discuss God, then, I must first start with the fact that I know that a long time ago there was a Big Bang. Yep! An invisible point exploded into what became the universe. But no one knows if our universe is the only one. There could have been lots of Big Bangs before us or in concert with us or after us. Science doesn't know, because science wasn't there. I also know that what I know is not necessarily what everyone knows. *"Knowing,"* the late David Viscott defined, *"is the truth from a certain perspective."* But let's look at the facts. I am college educated. I have lived 80% through the trials and tribulations of a relatively long life, being a strong family man for many years as well as a professional in architecture all that time. I'm fond of saying with a sly grin, *"My job is to help the rich realize their dreams!"* I'm passionate about reason, curiosity, adventure, an open mind, benevolence, empathy and the idea of continuing change. Over the past 13 years, I've read well over 700 books, including the Old and New Testaments, parts of the Quran, and many scientific books covering cosmology and quantum physics, albeit, mea culpa, written for the layman. A recent one was entitled *How it All Ends,* by Chris Imprey, meaning, of course, how science and Imprey *think* the whole Universe will end.

I also know that probably a good majority of the population of the world, which is, by the way, still increasing exponentially and according to Wikipedia has presently reached the much-too-large number of 7.4 billion *(more than half are poverty-stricken and there is already a world shortage of potable water),* still believe in the hereafter. And yet for most people this knowledge is discounted.

Now, where was I? Oh, yes! God, in relation to giving everyone a soul. Yes! God gave everybody a soul! But, about God: if there is a creative God,

1. *A priori: God made the Big Bang. (Visualize the entire explosion, galaxies, nebulae, quasars, clusters, etc. being a huge bubble or sphere);*
2. *A priori: Our galaxy, solar system and earth is within that sphere;*
3. *A priori: I'm in the sphere because something I'll call God made it; and*
4. *A priori: Parts of everything, rocks, water, plants, animals, fish, etc., are the substance of God's creation.*

(Some might make the case that the Big Bang and its result, macrocosm to microcosm, IS god! This idea, with which I do not necessarily agree or disagree, is beyond the

scope of this essay. Don't worry about it! It doesn't destroy this essay anyway.)

Or, let me put it another way. Our earth, which is still within the only known habitable sphere, is the natural product of supernatural forces, or of God, if you prefer.

5. *A priori: Our earth, (off, of which we cannot get) gave birth to everything on it, including you and me;*
6. *A priori: Therefore, all living creatures have earth as our only mother (presuming the universe is the father);*
7. *A priori: The earth and all its living offspring, then, are everyone's personal brothers or sisters; and,*
8. *A priori: To injure one is to injure all of our precious family.*

Now that the God thing is properly demystified, what about my soul? And here is Harold's answer, which to me, is a most powerful, delicate and seemingly indefinable concept:

The soul is ... *now I'm in trouble!*

Maybe I'd rather talk about what *Marge* thinks the soul is. She invented a graphic symbol that represents her most cherished beliefs. It consisted of a circle she called the *"universal force,"* and within that circle, she drew an oval that coincided with the perimeter of the circle at two of the closest points. This made equal and curved quarter-moons on each side of the oval, one quarter-moon symbolizing the intellect, the other symbolizing the physical. The remaining oval inside the circular is the spirit. The meaning? The symbol includes four things: a *universal force* that encompasses the *intellect* , the *physical* and the *spirit.*

I like this symbol and marvel at the sensitivity and philosophic state of mind of my wonderful wife and companion, Marge, who conceived it so long ago. Too bad I had to ruin it by asking, *"What about emotions?"* She thought about that for a little bit and decided emotions fell under *"physical."* I couldn't disagree, but had to further complicate and confuse matters by asking if her symbol also included personality. She replied I was getting too deep for her, she had other things to do, and get off her back!

But, returning to my own thoughts *(I couldn't let it alone),* I decided the living soul had to be within the living body. *(Where else could it be? Outside the body? That's ridiculous!)* After all, I reasoned, if I'm myself then I can look at me and thereby determine I am not somebody else. All other living people have souls and if I'm a living person, then I have a soul and it has to be within my body.

I've seen dead people. There's no soul there. What remains is only a physical reminder. I have no idea where their soul is or where mine will go. I hope heaven! But what and where is heaven? I hold my present thought;

We used to be nowhere.
Then we were born
and now we are somewhere.
A place called earth.
The earth is heaven.
When we die,
we go back to nowhere.

In any case, forget about where the soul goes for the moment. I'll discuss that later, and anyway it is obvious the soul is no longer in the physical part of the dead person.

9. *A priori: My living soul is within my living body - or it's not.*

I reasoned, somebody else's soul is not in my living body, unless I just *THINK* my soul is my own and are convinced somebody else's soul is my own when it's really not. I COULD BE DECEIVED! It could happen! For now, let's keep priori #9; My living soul is within my living body.

I determined my soul consisted of my living body plus every bit of information, large and small, that came into it from my five senses and from that special, miraculous inception of sperm into egg to the present time, including where I was located on the earth, and to whom I was born, and whether I came from a loving, medium, or abusive family. I decided personality, the capability for love, being extroverted, introverted, creative, having a potential for learning, being apathetic, lackadaisical, etc., was an important part, and since all personalities are as different as fingerprints, they must be an important part of my or any individual's soul.

Would I say my individual personality *WAS* my soul? Possibly! But that doesn't seem to cover it. What about automatic reactions, like catching a fork before it hits the floor, or automatically jumping to miss a snakebite, or risking your life and saving a child from being hit by a bus? What about instinctive moves? What about that universal sense that every human has of knowing what to do with no formal confirming? Are not these separate and distinct from what I would receive from my five senses? It seems that hunches and the universal consciousness would have to qualify as part of a person's soul. How could it not? All humans are born with the collective unconscious – that strange and mysterious universal consciousness that lies obscured and indistinct within the boundaries of the mind and body that at times seems miraculous, surprising and sometimes a challenging normalcy.

10. *A priori: The collective consciousness is part of the soul.*

I was reading about the brain the other day. The first part of the brain handles the autonomic nervous and bodily systems; breathing, heart beating, the workings of the liver, the circulatory system, kidneys, spleen, stomach, digestion, elimination, saliva, mucous, the fact that a broken bone will mend, but we can't grow a new liver, and all the things a healthy human never thinks about, but is so happy when it occurs, is also probably the main seat of the universal collective consciousness. But with everything working normally, I'm never concerned with my autonomic system or universal consciousness.

11. *A priori: The autonomic systems and universal consciousness are part of the soul.*

The next most primitive brain, the right brain, involves dreams, hunches, instincts, sense of knowing, putting things together, inspiration, the initial sense of creativity, the idea, etc. It is more primitive than the later left brain and if it came to a showdown, it would always win.

12. *A priori: The right brain is part of the soul.*

The last part of the brain to develop is the left brain. In very broad terms, it produces what the right brain has in mind. If the right brain gets an idea, such as Ford wanting to find an inexpensive means of transportation for the entire middle class, the left brain will decide how to do it – intelligent designs, industrial techniques, methods of mass production, advertising and delivery, etc. Without the left brain, no matter what the idea, nothing would be produced.

13. *A priori: The left brain is part of the soul.*

I'm fond of saying, the left brain is sometimes used for justifying the bad idea of the right brain. It sometimes makes logical sounding excuses, but that's neither here nor there.

What was I talking about? Oh, yes! The soul, what is it and where is it?

Well, we know it's in the body, so that's solved. And

when the body dies, it goes away, and only remains in the hearts and remembrances of those upon whom it made an impression. Where it physically goes is the subject of another essay.

Each individual is as different from any other individual as their fingerprints, so each soul is unique.

14. A priori: All souls are unique.

That means two or more people can't have the same soul. Twins, however, come close to having a single soul, but, yet, not quite, so I guess I could agree twin's souls are similar, but not exactly the same, and anyway, twins are well in the minority.

Since the brain is made of roughly three parts, and two parts plus the autonomic system and collective unconsciousness make up whoever the person is, the soul must involve those elements. When I hear of someone selling their soul or losing their soul or having lost their soul, it is terrifying to me, for they have lost or sold their very essence. They are gone; nothing but a dazed and wandering hunk of living flesh. When the soul is removed from it, it's probably the most hellish thing a person can do to themselves. They are now abandoned, not from just their mother, their father, their offspring, their dog or cat, or their work, but from themselves; the *incorporeal living essence* of who they are! In reality, someone who loses his soul has only added a different dimension to his or her existing soul. At any rate:

15. A priori: A soul is the most valuable possession it
    is possible to have.

So! The soul is within the living body, is unique, and is the most important possession any individual *(and I would add any animate or inanimate thing or entity)* can have.

Are we getting there? Oh, so slowly! And now that I've discussed the 15 priori', the pertinent and non-pertinent, I can think about what the soul is or is not. Here's the final production number, the answer to all, and I mean *ALL* of life's problems. It is as follows;

Harold's answer to what he thinks is a most powerful, delicate and seemingly unanswerable question: *WHAT IS THE SOUL?*

The soul is the *incorporeal essence of a person or living thing.*

WHAT? The same definition as Wikipedia's definition? We both thought I was going to come up with something different, surprising, and perhaps more shocking than Wikipedia. Well, I'm as disappointed as you are! I assumed I was different! So I guess we'll have to continue life with our own unique and never-to-be-duplicated souls and be proud of it, because in the last analysis, it couldn't get any better anyway. I have to be glad I've got one at all!

By the way, what does the word *"incorporeal"* mean? The Wik says, *"lacking a physical body or existing solely as a spirit."* It is also conceptually related to *"disembodied, ghostly, spiritual, intangible and ethereal."* That's believing! And believing falls into the above categories.

OK! I'm assuming, and I know I can't ASSUME a darn thing, that so many things go into defining a particular word, that society has agreed to skip all that and buy into a word like *"incorporeal"* that means all those same things. Don't hang the messenger! I don't make the rules! Nevertheless, me and the Wik agree:

The soul is the incorporeal essence
of a person or living thing.

THROUGH THAT DOOR
*(There is always a desire and a fear about opening up
a door that has been closed for such along time, but
introspection demands it and what is a courageous
person supposed to do?)*

Through that door,
beyond which lies
the darkness
of the unconscious mind,

I plunge my fist,

and reach through
the broken hole,
and close my hand,
grasping,
I know not what delight,
    or horror
I shall find,
    wriggling,
as I withdraw.

LOVE
(Since the bottom line on living is love, Harold, after living a considerable length of time on this earth, has arrived at a few thoughts.)

In life's last analysis, the ability to love is the greatest gift that may be bestowed. If I love myself I have a good start. If I'm active in my loving, loving will be returned, but that's not the reason to love. Loving and expecting something in return is not love, it's a bargain. Loving with no expectations is a reward in itself. It begins with the love of self.

In early childhood, an unresponsive caregiver, usually one lacking in its own self-love, fails to give the child the needed sense of worth. The child becomes *"needy"* of the love and looks to be loved by anyone in the vain hope that love from others will give it self-love. It's impossible to find someone to love me in the way I need to be loved and a pipe dream to hope someone else will *"understand"* and in his or her *"understanding"* cure my problem. Self-love cannot be handed to me. I have to have it within myself.

Normal parents who *"catch their child doing something right"* instead of *"catching them doing something wrong"* initiate self-love within the child. This good beginning is the foundation of the greatest gift that may be bestowed; one that establishes the miracle of being able to love others with no expectations of return.

Worldly problems exist by the large percentage of human species not having the ability to love, usually beginning with not being able to love themselves. That's how psychiatrists and psychologists came about. I have been twice to psychologists, once for nine months and the second time for two years. I see how they help their patients come to terms and make their way from unhappiness to happiness. A successful completion helps patients forgive themselves and love themselves, which ultimately allows them to love others with no expectation of reward and claim the greatest gift than can be bestowed.

The pattern is this: I first have to understand why I am the way I am.

In light of the Acid Sea of Reality, understanding leads to self-acceptance.

Acceptance leads to self-forgiveness.

Self-forgiveness leads to loving oneself.

No longer *"needy"* of love, I can now give love.

That's why the answer to problems is always love. I must remember to give self-esteem to others *(whether I've found it in myself or not?)*

Since self-approval and the feeling of personal worthiness transmit real power to the self, humans and living beings value it above everything else. *(Tell me if I'm wrong!)* If I want to contribute to the happiness of the world, I must complement when compliments are due, if only to tell a person, *"Good Job!"*

LIFE AFTER DEATH
(Yes, Harold thinks about life after death, or If we die again after our first death it may be death after death, but, then, if we come alive again, it would be life after life! Is he confused?)

DEATH AFTER DEATH makes no sense unless there is life after death and then only if those living after death, die to that world, then come back to live on earth or somewhere else as themselves, or as another living creature, and then died again, returned to earth and were reborn again, only to die and be reborn again, time after time, unending. Then we'd have DEATH AFTER LIFE AFTER DEATH AFTER LIFE AFTER DEATH, etc. throughout eternity. Death would be a transition between one kind of life *(or death)* and another. That could be exciting - unless I came back as a living creature where my lust for life would be in dire jeopardy.

Of course we could have LIFE AFTER DEATH without being reborn again. The deceased might exist forever in the place, wherever that is, where there is LIFE AFTER DEATH. They would have an eternity of happiness and be ecstatic talking and playing with their loved ones with no bills to pay and they'd always be young and healthy and smart; the children would not be into drugs, but well adjusted, and they'd always have something exciting to do, like a good bridge game, that keeps their juices flowing.

During the shortly-after-death-stage we can all see when we look in the coffin, that the body is no longer useful and already decaying. The spirit has long gone. At the point of death, we can say goodbye to the body, of which we have only one. We can say goodbye to taste, smell, hearing, sight and feeling. Some say that during death the spirit is drawn toward a bright light to a place where it is welcomed with open arms by a loving person or a loved one into an incredible, mind-blowing, other-worldly place, sometimes with incredible music. At this point their sight and hearing or imagination must still be in place. When I die, I'm prepared to be knocked out by ecstatic emotions, like smelling morning coffee, or coming upon a forgotten lake in Northern Canada with the smell of pine trees and fishy water, or blown by a freshened breeze announcing an approaching rainstorm with bright flashes of intermittent lightning, or discovering a later-life of love.

They say the mind, body and soul are interdependent and make a unity. Without the body, that leaves the mind and soul to relate to new experiences. Of course, my body is at least one-third of my life and that means the soul and mind would experience the glories of heaven all alone without their former vital companion. Were I the soul and mind, I'd really miss my body. I'd miss walking briskly through morning air, tasty meals, the thrill of a roller-coaster ride at Magic Mountain, the cool touch of the salt water ocean on my tanned skin, etc.

What happens to the autonomic nervous system of the mind? It controls breathing, pumping the heart, digestion and elimination of food, etc. I guess that's no longer necessary, and though it's part of the brain, it dies with the body. That which would be left would be language without speaking, listening without ears, pictures without eyes, ice cream without taste, and the aroma of fresh coffee without a nose, Ah! But the entity that passes on enters a new world and is reconstituted and miraculously reawakened to appreciate whatever new and wonderful happenings that occur.

According to the late psychologist, David Viscott, *"Belief is knowing something is so, whether it is or not."* While having tolerance for others who may not agree, I believe his definition.

One morning after a long jog, I was exercising on the back patio lifting hand weights over my head to exercise my arms when I spotted a tiny black creature no larger than a pinhead making its laborious way around the tiniest spec of sand and across what must have seemed to it, the vast expanses of my back patio. I had to stoop low to bring my face to within a foot of the creature to see him better. I could make out a hard black shell with a series of tiny legs propelling this minute being, perhaps an eighth of an inch per minute, on its incredible world and patio journey. I thought to myself, this bug hasn't any more idea why he's on the planet than I do. I felt a close attachment to this fellow creature, loved him and thought of the realm of the cosmos. We were both little creatures who were finding ourselves on a medium planet revolving around a medium sun. Was there really much difference between the two of us?

And if we were pals in my patio at this point in geologic time, why should I have everlasting life and the bug not? If there is life after death, why not for the bug, too? In fact why not for all living things, snakes and snails and puppy-dog tails. But if all living things went to heaven since they began life at least one half billion years ago, and their bodies and plants were strewn across the face of the earth making their evidence in coal and oil and granite and layer-after-layer of sedimentary rock and in the bottoms of dried up, landlocked oceans, that would make quite a few for one little 4-1/2 billion-year-old planet. And I guess, since the spirits of bodies of all living creatures are gone, heaven must be filled with hordes of spiritual no-see-ums, each with part of a mind and individual soul and no body. But where does this take place? It must be in the realm of the unknowable 96% of dark matter and energy.

Where else could it be? It can't be where we know it isn't. It must be somewhere we haven't looked, a place that is unknowable.

If there is life after death, it's reasonable that it's got to be for *all* living creatures, even mosquitoes and viruses, who have a right, like us, to life, liberty and the pursuit of happiness. If that's the case, all the dinosaurs spirits having lived on this planet for 135 million years before becoming extinct must take up a lot of spiritual space and they're probably crowded out by the total number of ants and ticks and spiders, the weight of which equals many times that of man.

So we must have a place out there that's special, perhaps in the realm of dark matter and dark energy. It might or might not be crowded with animal and plant spirits and that's only from our single planet. And I can't for the life of me see or touch or imagine them living unbelievably happy existences in the presence of whatever I can't see that may not be out there.

ROCKS

First, the Big Bang!
Then around the Bang
An expanding circle.
Let's call that Everything.
Within the Everything
Is the earth.
And upon the earth
Is ME!
Since the Big Bang
Made everything,
Of which I'm a part,
Then I was made
By the Big Bang.
Everything is the What.
I'm puzzled by the Why.

AUTOMATIC WRITING

(Upon occasion, Hal allows himself to free-think and so he sits at his computer to type his thoughts, whatever they are, and ponder things. He has no idea what will be produced by the end of the session, but this is the mystery and fun that will be revealed when he finishes.)

Well, here I am. I made it to eighty-four years old. Last night Marge threw me a party with Chris Lewi, Tom and Viv, Ernie and Camille and Amanda and the boys. There was much laughter and talking and good humor. Everyone seemed to have a good time. I got two books from Marge that I picked out with her at Barnes and Noble. One by Bill Cosby called *I Didn't Ask to be Born (But I'm Glad I Was)*, and another by Alexander McCall Smith, *Unforgettable Memories of Youth*. Chris gave me a political birthday card written to confuse, Amanda baked me an apple pie, and Viv and Tom will take us to see *The Artist*, a movie with a musical sound track and subtitles, but no audible words. I'll let myself know how it turns out the day after tomorrow. *(Sorry you won't know.)*

How did I feel about yesterday and how do I feel about my birthday today? I feel a lot of things. I feel a plethora of things. My old and good friend from my first architectural job said in a birthday letter that with my involvement in writing, artwork, and architecture, my head must be whirling with a lot of stuff. He doesn't know I've read at least thirty-six books a year for the past nineteen years. Reading keeps my mind active because I'm constantly revealing minimal portions of my personal ignorance. Of course, there's no end to anyone's personal ignorance, and yes, it's probably true that my head is filled with many things, hopefully only one thing at a time. But there is a benefit to that, because the basic tenets of art, writing and architecture are closely intertwined and what is true for one is generally true for the other.

I have more than my share of interest in the cosmos. That is, the big bang, stars, planets, nebulae, galaxies, the electromagnetic fields, black holes, The GOD particle, Higgs field, and the disturbing and invisible presence of dark matter and dark energy. I also am involved with tiny things like protons, neutrons, electrons and quarks, and I also enjoy writing about my own experiences with philosophy, psychology, how the brain works, and why people think weird things.

I am disturbed that the Christian Bible, Jewish Bible, and Koran have differing viewpoints and that many so-called devoutly religious worshippers take each sentence and thought so literally. In the books, it seems they've all but forgotten tolerance. If someone is not of the same group, they're an outsider and it's us against them that lead to violence and all the tortures of hell on earth. It seems it would be obvious to the religious that something is wrong. The Acid Sea of Reality seems to tell its message so clearly no one could possibly misunderstand.

A great portion of the adamantly involved can never give a different group a break. Nevertheless, the Acid Sea has spoken. All I need to do is open my eyes and see reality, such as religious wars that will stare me in the face. Apparently there is little hope for agreement in the near future and if I am to make friends with Reality, I have to make friends with the animosity of one group toward another.

The reality is that even though all children of the world, black, white, yellow, beige, etc., arrive out of a similar womb, they are doomed or blessed by the natural occurrence of how they are raised, at least for the first ten formative years of their lives. They are young and ready to be warped according to parental thoughts and beliefs and circumstances of their local environment.

I must conclude, like the advanced animal I am, that we're just another species, perhaps, much like the chimpanzee whose DNA is 97% identical to human DNA. Chimps are designed to guard their territory with their life, specifically by killing another chimp or chimps that cross that territorial line. Sharing or compassion never seems to occur to them. They are built to act violently as instinctually or automatically as a cat plays with a mouse or a coyote leaps on an unsuspecting rabbit.

Even though we're top of the line, it seems we don't think of ourselves as just another species. There seems to be the thought that humans are divine creatures made in the image of God and that our humanness is far above that of the lowly animals. What are we thinking? That we're in an entirely different category? I don't even have to ask, *"Are we?"* Because the Acid Sea continually reminds me that the population explosion has doubled in the past 30 years, the ozone layer continues diminishing, the massive Greenland and North Pole icebergs continue to melt destroying the habitat of polar bears. The proliferation of oil products are releasing vast quantities of carbon into the atmosphere exacerbating global warming, the natural forests are continuing to be cut, including those trees that produce our vital life-giving oxygen and massive numbers of animal species continue going extinct. Pollution of the ocean by oil spills and idiotic fishing methods move along by scraping the bottom of the oceans, the origin of edible sea-life, a vital source of our food, is being diminished, and the rapidly growing need for clean, fresh water, and the fact that over half the earth's population lives in a state of ignorance and poverty is excessively deplorable, not to speak of the abominable lack of world education.

I'd say the human species, while it is God-like in the basic sense, the actual Sea of Reality is far from being God-like in the humanitarian sense. It seems to be our reason that vulnerable part of our brain that contains the only hope of saving the planet, is not sufficiently developed, and the instincts of greed, family preservation, personal comfort, etc., are most predominant. So, where does that get us? Where does that get me? There seems to be little I can do about the earth's problems.

Reading the book called, _How it All Ends_, which discusses the end of our sun, earth, planets, galaxies, nebulae, and the entire universe including the Big Bang, I have learned our planet will survive another four-and-a-half billion years before it is enveloped by the increasing size of our dying sun. Other reading tells me that if our privileged planet were to start all over again, it probably would not develop a creature as intelligent and creative as our own human species. The dinosaurs lived well over a hundred and thirty-five million years until their extinction sixty-five million years ago, caused by an asteroid hitting the Yucatan Peninsula. If it had missed the earth, dinosaurs would still be ruling the planet and miniature mammals would be living in holes to avoid the reptilian giants and their own extinction.

It's my philosophy that life must be lived in process and context. We'll build a hybrid car because gas prices are too high. Building a gas-guzzler when fuel is limited doesn't work. I want to live the process of my life within the context of what's going on around me. I made it to eighty-four. How am I? I'll tell you. I don't have the energetic body I had when I was ten years younger. My kids are ten years older and since time is change, things have changed with children and friends. So, it's time to go with Marge and have a chile relleno.

FISH WITH A WISH

For a million years
  I have lived in the sea.
I have eaten a billion other fish
  to survive.
I have escaped a million fish
  who would have eaten me.
My species is in jeopardy.
  I know what it is
that I must do
  to stay alive.
I know what nature
  will have me do
to survive.
  And so I find myself
cast on shore
  a fish
with a wish
  to stay alive.

INERTIA

(Sometimes the Self doesn't feel well which can be a positive sign. Not feeling well is really the marker for change. Portions of the left brain have the miraculous ability to examine the past and speculate on the future. It's our one source of figuring things out for ourselves. Not feeling well is a signal I have to break the INERTIA within myself. To do this I must change how I <u>think</u> about things, which will have a direct affect upon how I <u>feel</u> about things.)

Is the bulldozer of my life dead at the foot of life's immovable rock? Does my 20 pound line break when hooking life's whale? Has the side of my ship been ripped stem to stern by the impenetrable iceberg of my life? Has my freight train jumped the track and plowed through the city of my dreams? What happens when the irresistible force meets the immovable object?

Inertia, my friends, inertia!

(The tendency of a body to resist acceleration or to remain at rest or, if in motion, to stay in motion in a straight line unless acted on by an outside force.)

Yes, those are the parts of physical inertia. *"Heck!"* You say, *"I could have told you that!"* Yesterday I picked up a pencil under my desk and bumped my head on the bottom of the table. My head was moving, but the table wasn't. Or my heavy leg moves fast and kicks a light football that zooms for sixty yards and almost out of sight. *(I can dream, can't I?)* It's not nice to cross the double line *"and not see the truck."*

But we're talking physical inertia here. What about mental inertia? As we saw in the discussion on the self, the unconscious or elephant mind is huge and will not easily change. It has INERTIA! It can only be changed if the five senses and the conscious mind, the rider, make it understand it's more advisable to change than not. A big ship will not come around like a catamaran. A chicken can't pressure a lair of foxes.

If you've ever dealt with a city's building department, you know of bureaucratic inertia. How hard is that to change? Or governmental inertia! It takes forever for the majority to vote and the rules to change. Even the difficulty of changing the group's mind at a property owner's association meeting is next to impossible. Why is that so?

> *Purpose and intent*
> *was not carefully thought out,*
> *or hasn't kept up with the times,*
> *or has been mindlessly lost.*

Solutions lie within the initial purpose and intent. The purpose and intent of a city's building department is to protect innocent people from being taken advantage of, to make things safe and to establish rules about all conditions in the area. Like law enforcement, if they didn't make rules, society would suffer. Without rules, things would be in chaos and all would suffer. Sorry, folks, that's the way of the Acid Sea of Reality. Make friends with reality! Don't kill the messenger! I speak the truth! For me to make a societal change as a single person would be like me running out into a stampeding buffalo herd heading for destruction at the brink of a canyon, waving my arms and shouting, *"STOP!"*

Governmental inertia is the same thing only bigger; people making rules to protect the rights of others so people don't get hurt. We're dealing with all America, here, folks, not a lunch counter group. There is inertia in property owner's association groups and even with a man and wife, in fact for any group larger than one, we have group inertia. Where does it come from? The willful actions are those of a group. You can't fight city hall. Fixing mental inertia can be like fighting city hall.

The solution lies within the purpose and intent. That means I must be conscious of my purposes, while not forgetting my own mental inertia. If things aren't working, why? How do I change? It's like working for change within the government, or building department, or property owner's association, or a single person like my wife or my wife's husband, me. I can't, like the well-intentioned savior when he senses something is drastically out of place, run out in the middle of a stampeding herd of buffalo heading for the drop-off and certain death and shout, *"STOP! No! No! No!"* I'd get trampled and die!

The better way is to join the herd telling each buffalo there's a steep drop ahead and urge them to pass it on. Then tell another buffalo and tell him to pass it on, and so on, and so on. I might tell enough buffalo so the word permeates the herd and they swerve just in time to miss the deadly fall. Then again, I may save most, but the rest goes over, then again, I may be too late, altogether, and the whole herd goes over to the last calf. Life is not perfect, so says the Acid Sea of Reality. Then, if I don't go off the cliff with them, I shrug and say, *"Sorry!"*

So, how do I change mental inertia? First I have to know something is wrong, for instance my wife doesn't talk to me anymore and I've lost my job. My kids tell stories behind my back, etc. I'll say to myself. *"Say! Things are not right, here! I've no money and I'm not happy!"* This is a warning to change my behavior or change my thinking. Hopefully, pain will motivate and I'll heal myself by finding new purposes and intents and advertising to myself all the correct things. In other words, advertise my way to mental health!

How do I do that? I must go back to original purposes and intents; back to childhood, if necessary, to discover if, in the present light of examination, the original purposes and intents were correct. If the solution is contained among the original purposes and intents of my life and things are not going well, perhaps those purposes and intents, or the lack of them, must be investigated. To win the battle, I must know the enemy, which means standing up and facing the Acid Sea of Reality. If the purpose and intent of the enemy was misdirected or foul, I must understand this, form a new purpose and intent, and live by that.

The accumulation of all information that has arrived through my five senses for a lifetime and the feelings aroused are like the mass of bureaucratic, or governmental, or property owner's association rules. I must treat them like a herd of stampeding buffalo, go among them each, spread the proper word as derived from my new purposes and intents in order to get them to swerve and not go off the cliff. Personal attention to each problem for as long as it takes, will lead me to sanity and happiness. *"Quick, Watson. The game's afoot!"*

EMERGING

(Harold decided to come out! How could he remain in Fantasy when he could have that marvelous experience of making friends with Reality. Of course, making friends with Reality sometimes forces him to enter the Acid Sea in order to reap the miraculous benefit. Buried under layers of defenses, heredity, the complex mental language of the human brain, the incomprehensible collective unconscious and God knows what else, a portion of Harold's deepest self, after years of therapy and continual encouragement, was cautiously about to make itself known. He dared to enter Reality!)

> *Emerging, then,*
> *from the grass,*
> *tall, green, luxuriant,*
> *shifting, irregular,*
> *dark, it moved,*
> *uncertain,*
> *a pawn in the wind.*
> *it moved in the dark,*
> *as stars,*
> *piercing the back of night*
> *gently puncture*
> *a violet drop.*

The green grass glowing; a representation of a fresh young world teeming with health and energy; an enthusiastic living backdrop with power to allow anything to survive.

> *The green grass growing,*
> *illuminated from within,*
> *spent its weary force,*
> *wavering then blowing*

steady, then bending,
flowing then stopping,
in the cool night wind.

And fearful did it finally arrive, to live in the powerful world for the first time after so many years. Forever hidden, buried, afraid, and hoping it will be a happy place, but as yet unable to see, look, or experience its hoped-for wonderfulness. A new part of himself is coming into consciousness - an unimaginable heaven.

And emerging therefrom,
furry and black
with soft yellow eyes,
and curved black claws,
vicious, yet gentle,
but fearful,
the creature came forth,
and moving and twitching the grass,
made its meticulous way
into the violent night.

A hidden part of himself comes fearfully into the world, presumably the one known by everyone else. His once-fearful being might move through love, fear, hope and knowledge and learn to cope with life now to be experienced on a larger scale. A portion of his real self is now available to help him live a good and productive life.

PRAYER

(Harold thought a person praying a lot was just a person hoping a lot and prayers equaled hopes. If a person prayed for his elderly father with a painful illness to live for an unspecified time, he'd just be hoping a lot that his father would live longer for his own sake even if, perhaps, blocking his father's feeling of extreme discomfort and even his father's wish to die.)

But that brings to mind the subject of HOW the individual phrases the prayer.

I pray for him to live. I pray he will have an easy death. I pray he will be able to stand the pain, I pray he will survive despite his painful illness. I pray that what happens is what he wants to have happen. I pray what I want to happen will happen. I pray he won't die 'til Tuesday. I pray his daughter gets to see him before he dies, etc. etc., etc.

So, how one prays becomes important and its effects become significant. All kinds of people pray differently, some self-serving, some compassionate, some over-sensitive, some who will gain monetarily, either with his life or with his death and a multitude of unconscious/ conscious reasons in this irrevocable, on-going process called life. We are as different as our fingerprints. Perhaps this subject is too big for me.

I've heard that people in intense pain are sometimes encouraged to continue living because their loved one needs them to keep living. Praying for an elderly father to continue living a painful, terminal life occasions two messages. (1) Praying for your father to continue to live in pain and (2) Praying for him to be alive a while longer because the prayer-giver could not give him up.

A better prayer might be to allow the wishes of the almost-dead to prevail – unless you don't trust his decisions are in his best interests. But that's a subjective of choice, isn't it so? If it were me, how could I be sure I was doing the reasonable thing? I would be like many others in this time and place, that decisions for another's life are heavy to make.

But that only considers one kind of prayer. How about being in a play for your first time on stage and praying you remember the lines. *"I pray I'll know my lines and do my business properly and that other actors and I will make the play a success."* Or if waiting for the big game to begin. *"I pray I do well and that our team plays valiantly and we win the big game!"* Why pray? Because I'll feel I've done my best for myself and the team; we are smarter and better conditioned than our opponents and can overcome adversity. In other words, *"I and our team are better!"* Of course the other side is praying for the same thing, so who's to judge? Are we grading the prayer or the game's outcome? Is praying helpful or is it just hoping a lot? Is prayer wishful thinking?

Praying puts into words what he or she wants to happen. This is a good thing. I know that learning and thinking is good. Thinking and saying is better. Thinking, saying and writing it down is even better, and thinking, saying, writing it down, and doing it is the best. So, I'd have to say about prayer that thinking and saying is better than just thinking.

It's my contention that prayers need to be acknowledged by those who are prayed for and otherwise are useless. That is, if the other person or community or group or the world hasn't heard the nature of the prayers, they do little good. If masses of Afghanistan people pray for American soldiers to leave their country, their prayers are useless, unless they are heard by Americans and help change the soldiers' minds. I need to know Afghans are praying for Americans to leave their country so I can use my head and decide whether or not to recall our troops. *"It's important to examine the nature of the sources."* It may be my judgment for the greater good of the nations for the troops to stay. Maybe my decision is better for them in the long run than what they propose. Or maybe it's not and we need more information.

It recently was necessary for a popular female television host to enter the hospital for a stem-cell transplant. *(Deceased bone marrow no longer produces healthy blood cells and must be thoroughly killed by radiation, then new, healthy cells from another owner are injected.)* By most standards it's a difficult operation. In this case, thousands of her viewers prayed for her recovery and she was blatantly aware of that fact. I'm sure the support of her fans was a great emotional help in her recovery. I do not deny that prayers of support emotionally help anyone to face powerful difficulties.

Then, there are wars that are really, really, really the big game; an activity where the players/soldiers, their families and officers on both sides are praying for victory. They don't want to get killed, they've got better things to do, and it's the least to say it's an inconvenience and hardship for their loved ones. This reminds me of the saying, *"Pray, but keep your powder dry."* What does that mean? For an effective prayer and best success of the final outcome, I must do everything in my power for its accomplishment. I remember, *"God helps those who help themselves."* I love the humorous biblical quotation my deceased friend, Rick Davidson and I invented, *"To really knoweth a man, looketh not at what he say he gonna do, but looketh at what he already done do."* What a man does, he achieves or not. What he says he'll do is suspect. I've always linked praying to saying rather than doing. I still believe saying has nothing to do with *"keeping your powder dry."*

Praying can be seen as an act of desperation. For example, this morning there were a hundred or so bees busily gathering sugar from fallen grapes that dropped from our overhanging trellis. Though most bees buzzed and hummed and returned to their hive, a few dipped for a drink into a bowl of clean water I'd put out for the birds. Bees are very light and after drinking, the water's surface tension allows them to fly away, but a few legs, perhaps having been dipped too gustily from their airborne flight, broke the water's surface tension and underlying water saturated their bellies. Four bees got stuck. They swam with their legs and buzzed with their wings in a desperate attempt to reach the side or lift themselves into the air. Nevertheless, their situation was hopeless. They'd exhausted their resources and it was time for the bees to pray. Tomorrow I'd find lifeless bees on the bottom of the water bowl. But their prayers were answered, this 152 pound creature from another world loaded with energy and desire to interrupt his fine day, dipped dry leaves under the bees and dropped them to safety on the grass where they dried themselves. The bees presumably went about their bee-like existence in a normal way. If they had been capable and prayed to the universal powers, there occurred a wild bolt from the sky and their prayers were answered! Great Forces have been known to send miracles. How unlikely is that?

But, regarding wartime experiences, *"There are no atheists in foxholes."* This means there's a lot of praying going on down there. When death is full upon a soldier, what are the alternatives? When he's done everything he can think of to save himself and has exhausted his creativity, intelligence, and physical abilities, and he is tired to the bone, and the war has worn away his spirit, what is there left to do but pray? *"He's kept his powder dry."* He's in a mortally desperate situation and praying to God, if religious, or to the universal force if not to God, or to some all-powerful force totally beyond his comprehension. God or the universal force or fate or some force of which we know almost nothing, holds his only hope. He will probably die, but the great forces have been known to send miracles.

The Marines suddenly arrive. Heavy rain stops the bombing, a bomb misses, a meteor streaks from outer space and plummets into the enemy.

It's possible! It could happen! Giving hope where there is no reason for hope is the object of such a prayer. I'd probably die anyway, but I'd pray to the collective unconscious and every unseen, impossible, unknowledgeable and unexpected source to be my savior. It's happened!

Though I've not verbalized them to friends, acquaintances or the public, there are certain things for which I've been hoping. My hope is so strong; I feel I AM the prayer or hope. I address my hopes and prayers to God or the Universal Force - those unseen, unimaginable, unknowledgeable powers that run fate-like through the known world. Keeping my powder dry, requires I DO SOMETHING! I contribute whatever I can afford to my choice of helpful organizations. I hope for reliance on wind and solar power and sources other than fossil or nuclear fuels for world energy. I hope for cleansing our polluted air and oceans and streams; for the re-establishment of the decimated forests; for control of the exponential rise of human population, for total reduction of genocidal governments and the increase of what I consider to be the flowers of any country, the schools; I hope for new developments in medicine, drugs, dentistry, biology, microbiology, quantum physics, astronomy, and space exploration, for the medical profession and organizations like the World Wildlife Fund or Save the Whales to ease the pain of disease and abnormalities. Like the typical Miss Universe contestant, I also hope and pray for world peace.

Then, there are the standard prayers

1 - Thou shalt have no other Gods before me.
   If God is the universal force, I have no other God.
2 - Thou shalt make no carved images.
   It's hard to make a carving of the universal force.
   The world has already pretty well been carved.
3 - Thou shalt not take the Lord's name in vain.
   It makes little difference to swear in its name
   because the universal force, as fate, is incapable of
   caring.
4 - Thou shalt remember the Sabbath day.
   I enjoy taking a time out once a week to rest from
   normal activities. Doing different things brings me a
   broader enlightenment and better perspective on
   my life. There was and is no Sabbath for the
   universal force. It continues to pursue its relentless
   course throughout eternity.
5 - Thou shalt honor thy father and mother.
   By all standards, I had outstanding parents, felt
   loved, and shall always honor them.
6 - Thou shalt commit no murder.
   This is ridiculous! I don't need to pray not to kill
   somebody. It's the last thing on my mind, but I
   suppose it depends on the circumstances. If
   someone purposely injures my kid, within the limits
   of the law, I'll not be responsible for what I do.
   Sometimes murder is justified. If my family is

threatened, I'll defend it and keep my powder dry.

7 - Thou shalt not commit adultery.

I've got to bend on that one. My present wife and I left troubled twenty-five year marriages. We each had made lifetime commitments far before we were emotionally ready. In our new marriage, we've had over thirty-four years of wedded enjoyment with seven children and eight grandchildren, all unified and happy. Correcting a bad mistake that has life-long negative consequences must be given fair evaluation.

8 - Thou shalt not steal.

I will not, but if I'm ready to die from lack of food and water, I'd steal. But, OK, I'm a fortunate man. I've got a job and family and enough so stealing is not necessary.

9 - Thou shalt not bear false witness.

Bearing false witness is bad. It doesn't agree with an agreeable admonition, "Do unto others as you would have them do unto you." Bearing false witness blackens both persons and can do harm. I'll go along with this one.

10 - Thou shalt not covet thy neighbor's wife.

I'll have to give that one a mea-culpa because I did fall in love with another's wife and in return, she fell in love with another's husband. Eventually, everyone was happier including the divorced spouses and their children. Somewhere there should be a commandment, "Thou shalt learn from one's mistakes and correct them if you can."

Now I'd like to interpret a prayer my mother taught me when as a little child:

> *"Now I lay me down to sleep,*
> *I pray the Lord my soul to keep;*
> *If I should die before I wake,*
> *I pray the Lord my soul to take."*

Interpretation:

"Now I lay me down to sleep,
> *I'm being put to bed.*

I pray the Lord my soul to keep;
> *Even though I've just begun my life, I'm praying or*
> *asking or hoping that some powerful personage that I*
> *don't know will keep my soul for me, if I have a soul,*
> *because, evidently I couldn't keep it myself and mom*
> *and dad aren't up to it.*

If I should die before I wake,
> *I speculate about dying before morning even though*
> *mom and dad thought I'd probably make it through*
> *the night. Death at five years old was far beyond my*
> *imagination and when they described it as not being in*
> *the world anymore, it scared the heck out of me.*

I pray the Lord my soul to take."
> *I was encouraged to verbalize that it was my prayer,*
> *hope, and desire that IF, as a youngster, I were to pass*
> *on to a better world, the powerful personage whom*
> *I don't know would accept my soul, which I was not*
> *sure what one was, and that I'd be somehow better off.*

Though a child cannot grasp the meaning of the poem, the loving way it's presented has its positive affect. It is usually clear that the child is worthy of being loved. In later life and for those who are then better able to understand the meaning of prayers, it allows the one who prays to clarify his/her subject. Prayer is similar to hope, but in our society carries more weight. It can be intimate, or altruistic, or selfish, or desperate, but in every case clarifies the thoughts, feelings and position of the one who prays. It more firmly establishes the person's wants and desires that provoke an action to achieve that which is desired.

It's certain that it is beneficial in the majority of cases, that if the ill, injured, or unhappy person knows he or she is being prayed for, he or she knows those praying persons care for them and the ill or unhappy, knowing they are cared for to whatever the degree, encourages self worth and a greater ability to cure themselves. A prayer that is hoping, wishing, praying or desiring of a positive outcome is extremely beneficial to the less than fortunate person.

EMANUEL

(Harold knows he has inherited a miraculous GOD
WITHIN or spirit from the universal creative forces
and calls out to Emanuel to make this
knowledge a reality.)

EMANUEL
Where are you?
Leaping from a cloud,
tiny stick-figure,
smaller than the sun,
gleefully falling,
arms awry,
into another billowy bed?
You're not dead!

EMANUEL!
Come out now.
I see you there,
seaweed in your hair,
playing with seashells
and patterns of sunlight
on jewel-strewn sand
in a saltwater land.

EMANUEL!
Is that you
that I barely see,
through swamp mist,
drifting, silvery,
atop the Cypress tree,
beckoning me?

EMANUEL!
Please talk to me.
You with eyes
that see through mine.
You, whose soul
knows all souls.
You, with time
that knows no time.
Tell me I belong to you.
Tell me you love me, too.
Show me again
the variety and range
of what I long to do.

TOLERANCE
(To better make a point, Harold speaks in parables.)

"I see blowing up the world as a vast mistake." Harold made the preceding quote to his friends over coffee on November 9, 1981. Perhaps it wasn't his greatest insight, but it was the best for the day.

Upon hearing this statement, some of the friends, hands covering their mouths, sniggled. Others laughed out loud at the obviousness of this thought. One intelligent person asked, *"For whom?"* Meaning for whom would it be a mistake?

Harold replied, *"Why, for everybody."*

When asked to elucidate, he said *"Everybody would be dead because there would be no land to stand on, nor forests or trees or oceans or streams of fish or birds. There might be clouds, however, but not the same kind as we see in the heavens today."*

Someone asked, *"How did you come to know all this?"*

Harold replied, *"It came to me in a flash while waiting for the stoplight to change."*

One of the guests, sipping her coffee, then asked, *"What can we do about it?"*

Harold said, *"I guess we'll all just have to see the other person's point of view, value it a as a rarity, and protect it as if it were a priceless jewel."*

"Why do that?" Cried those who were or weren't listening.

Harold replied, *"Because mankind has already tried NOT listening to other's points of view and the world is about to make a vast mistake. Sometimes our own point of view can blur or even obliterate the others point of view."*

Groaning and sighing arose from those who heard Roy's answer as they shifted their weight, first to this foot then to that. *"Yeah, but …. Yeah, but …. Yeah, but …"* said one intelligent person and followed each *"Yeah, but …"* with a reasonable question like, *"What if I see others' points of view and value them as a rarity, but they don't see my points of view and value them as a rarity?"*

Harold proceeded with the following story:

A man called up his brother on the phone, but his brother wouldn't answer, so he tried and tried until, for whatever reason, the brother did answer the phone and then they communicated.

"What did they say to each other?" Said a little boy standing nearby.

"I don't know. Said Harold. "But the moral is, if you can't communicate right this moment, you must keep trying."

"Woof! Woof! That makes sense!" Barked a dog, taking off his hat and scratching his head with one paw. People threw pencils and napkins at the dog until, yelping, he ran out of the house.

"I see blowing up the world as a vast mistake." This statement by Harold on November 9, 1981 was written on a piece of paper by Roy's wife along with his opinion that, in order to keep our beautiful world, others' points of view are going to have to be seen as a rarity and protected as we would protect a priceless jewel.

(With regard to Carl Rogers, who, in his paper, Do We Need "A" Reality? So clearly developed this thought. From <u>*A Way of Being*</u>*, Houghton Mifflin Company, Boston, MA, 1980, pp 96-108) Note: This essay is from* <u>*Book of Words*</u> *with permission of the author, Doug Rucker, Vilimapubco publishing company)*

Explanation: Being willing to discuss matters holds the door open to discussion that leads, hopefully, to resolution. Not to invite serious discussion is to invite non-understanding. Non-understanding leads to greater conflict that gives birth to the *"enemy."* Enemies lead to the dehumanizing aspects of war. Keeping the door open to discussion humanizes humans leading, hopefully, to peace.

I REACH AND REACHING, REACH

I am next to,
but not quite.

I search inside.
I sink to depths,
I look within.

Round, red balls
of soft red fire
cling to the edge
of a black burnt tree
with leaves as green
and thick and green,
or greener.

This, I find
and nothing more.

I must descend
to a greater depth.

To find whatever
I know I'll find.

I must reach and reach,
and reaching,
reach.

MYSELF

(Harold must have asked," Where is it? It seems so obvious to look down and see your body and limbs. There is no one without a self! But there are other forms of knowing self than just looking. Nevertheless, he can start there.)

When I ask where is my *'self'*, I point to a region around my navel, not that the navel has anything to do with it. It may be me, but it's only a part. My fingernails are also part of me as are my hair, ears, kneecap, blood vessels, and brains. I might as well have pointed to those and said they were myself, but they are not the complete self.

When I say self, I don't mean everything except my little toe or the fingernail on my left hand, I mean all of me including the parts that are mental and emotional and spiritual. In combination, all those parts that make the one, glorious, miraculous *me*. My physical self includes the sympathetic nervous system controlling parts of me I rarely think about; the function of heart, lungs, liver, and the inner organs, though they play a strong part in defining self, for the present time, I'm leaving them out.

All parts of my physical, emotional, mental and spiritual life, must work. It's great if a Mercedes Benz goes places and does things, but if the water hose is broken, the car might be pretty, but it ain't goin' nowhere. All parts, physical, emotional, mental and spiritual, then, belong to me and are part of my self. They're not parts of somebody else.

Other than the workings of the sympathetic nervous system, my seeable, feelable physical being, self, are really broken into two categories, the conscious and unconscious. Jonathan Haidt, in his book called *The Happiness Hypothesis*, provides a brilliant metaphor between the conscious and unconscious minds. I quote Andy Smith who tells me that Haidt likens the conscious and unconscious mind to rider and elephant.

> *"The rider represents the controlled processes of the mind, the planning and reasoning that takes place one step at a time in conscious awareness, while the elephant represents the hundreds of automatic operations we carry out every second outside of conscious awareness. It includes emotions, gut feelings, and visceral responses, etc."*

Rather than taking a giant leap to any instant conclusion, I always tell my kids to talk all around a subject and examine its relationships before making a judgment or decision. This allows them to make mindful judgments or decisions that keeps their minds open and stimulates awareness - the key to a happy life.

Following my own advice, then, I'm going to jump to the subject of belief whose prerequisite is the feeling of knowing. My self is dependent on what I feel I know and what I feel I know is indicative of what I believe. Feeling of knowing = believing. It's possible if not probable that someone can Know something beyond a doubt and yet it doesn't Feel right. *(A young mother letting her child cry itself to sleep at 2 A.M. Riding alone in an untethered balloon and being swept along by a stout wind, flying with a young pilot in a small plane over the Rockies.)* He or she Knows something is true, yet can't fully Feel it or believe it's right.

Deceased psychologist, David Viscott, stated that people can be in a state of *"Knowing is the truth from a certain perspective."* That means I can know something is right when it's utterly wrong. The Republicans knew they'd win the 2012 presidential election, but they were wrong. I guess knowing something is right when it's wrong is better than not having given the problem any thought at all. In my own special viewpoint, knowledge is life and ignorance is death, so, if I'm to know my self and what I know = what I believe is the most vital part of who I think I am.

Knowing, rather than the feeling of knowing, arises from the less powerful conscious mind – the rider of the elephant. The feeling of knowing comes from the more powerful elephant. *(Unconscious mind)* Sometimes the rider *(conscious mind)* and the elephant *(unconscious mind)* are in concert and then a person has belief.

How do I get to know what I believe? Let's start with the easy things. I feel I know the sun comes up every morning and when it rains the flowers are wet. I feel I know it is better to come in out of the cold. There are many things we all know and so with those, we have the feeling of knowing. Other than the sun, moon and stars, there's a dichotomy of beliefs that challenge what I think I know; abortion *(Roe vs. Wade),* Clinton, Trump, ISIS wars, pollution, global warming, Wall Street, health care, or whether the cat's better in or out at night.

Then there are beliefs I cannot help having. I can't help unconditionally loving my kids. I can't help being repulsed by dog poo-poo. Tough folks, but that's the way it is. A new mother can't help loving her new son or daughter. She loves her baby unconditionally whether she likes it or not. That's the way it is! It's fate! In both cases the feeling of knowing is first and those Feelings come directly from the more powerful elephant or unconscious mind. Nature has decreed it so! It cannot be otherwise! *"Give it up for fate!"*

I have to assume, we all know about these feelings

where there is no doubt. But what about the more controversial stuff? Why do we find so much difficulty in getting the feeling of knowing about the more contentious questions? I have to admit, I'm a *percentage* kind of guy who tries to adapt to a world in constant change.

I feel I know Obama's Presidency is good about 80% because I feel I know he's a true statesman that believes in living relative to the world including family, Congress, Senate, Supreme Court, Republicans, Democrats, CIA, FBI, etc. I feel I know he will do anything he feels is right most of these changing times.

I feel I know that everything exists in relationship to everything else from the Big Bang to the planet earth to the solidity of the six quarks that inhabit the proton. Abortion, depending on conditions, is wrong most of the time, but I can't leave the prospective mother out. In making judgments and deciding about things, I feel I know about everything from a percentage and relative point of view in changing times.

But where does the self figure in all this? Since self is believing what one knows, which is the feeling of knowing, I have to discuss how anyone arrives at the feeling of knowing .

In Robert A. Burton, M.D.'s book, *On Being Certain*, he discusses the role of learning that occurs in the brain's synapses. Learning can only arrive through our five senses; seeing, hearing, tasting, feeling and smelling. When we're born, these are our only receptors. There are no other learning methods. Baby feels and tastes the milk in her mother's breast, giggles when tickled, responds to pleasant sounds, is fascinated by colored lights and is afraid of falling and loud noises. Project the same thing from life to death and the process is the same, ad infinitum, and all the senses are relative to each other and to what's happening at the time.

In a most simplified explanation, the brain is the place that processes all the new material from the five senses. Pain does not automatically go to the knee or elbow or any other part of the body. It's hard-wired specifically to go to the brain.

What is to be learned, therefore, arrives in the brain through the senses in the form of pre-synaptic neurons that enter what is called the axon terminal. The axon terminal is a kind of jumping off place for the would-be neurons to leap, for that is literally what it is designed to do, jump across the gap called the synoptic cleft. It leaps or flows or is electrically transmitted or moves across a narrow gap. What the gap or breach is made of, I'll have to refer you to further study. I don't think its air. Saltwater brain goo?

Across the gap is the dendrite, a membrane that contains receptors waiting to absorb the neurons' new information. The gap or synaptic cleft is a kind of a filtering system that scans the incoming material, deciding what is to be learned and what is not.

The receptors are a product of a lifetime of experiences received through my five senses and being representative of my subconscious, will pick and choose what I will learn and what I will not.

If a teacher shows me a finished equation, the answer's there, but I'll not understand it unless I'm motivated to study hard. Even so, I may not get it because, unlike Stephen Hawking, I'm not good at math. The unconscious decides what I will learn easily or uneasily and what I will not. My daughter loves dogs and dogs love her and when she sees a dog it wags its tail and there is an instant bond. I, on the other hand, was bitten on my side at six years old by a large German Shepherd and much later, on the wrist by another large dog. I am more wary and distrustful and see dogs with a different eye than my daughter. At least my subconscious does. These are examples of how my or anyone's subconscious can color an attitude toward incoming information and determine through the receptors what I will learn. It actually restricts information from coming in and thereby restricts learning. A tremendous effort would have to be made to free myself of those ingrown attitudes and implicitly trust dogs again. Considering my personality and character and lack of importance to me, I won't.

That means, though great quantities of information have arrived, what I actually learned is what my unconscious or receptors allowed. This is part of the real me and that is part of my real self, my lumbering elephant with its built in attitude, ability or disability to learn, talent, capability, personality, likes, dislikes, fears, prejudices, loves, and all the information that it has heretofore accepted. All the information that has entered my brain has been filtered through the synaptic cleft controlled by its boss, the *unconscious*, and learned or not learned by the *conscious*. Attached to the unconscious are its accessories, the physical self and the conscious mind. My self is all three, but the massive, controlling self is the sleeping giant, the elephant part of me or unconscious mind.

A word about the rider. I consider life an adventure. The greatest adventures lie within the realm of my own personal ignorance. Therefore, I want to explore the realm of my own personal ignorance while having a strong curiosity and keeping a welcoming heart and open mind. I don't want to be caught sleeping while a miracle is occurring right outside the window. An open mind stimulates my unconscious, even though it may be injured through bad things I learned or happened in the past. These can be mitigated by new information gathered by my rider, the conscious mind, and I will try to feed my self good things on a daily basis that will provide me with happy memories.

MING AND MANG

(Harold got divorced! Too bad! It was not something he intended, nor could he have avoided, but reality stared him in the face. This was part of his, and perhaps others' personal Acid Sea of Reality.)

Mang is huge with fire for eyes,
with stones for feet,
and hooks for hands.
He walks on tree-stump legs,
and slices clouds
with a black-night sword.
Ming, with armored jaw
and iron-spiked toes,
presses them deep
in the river's mud,
her passions in cycles,
weak as a willow,
strong as a storm,
awaits the attack.
Mang advances, sword held high.
Ming awaits, afraid to die.
The clatter of battle
shatters all peace.
The sun hangs limp.
The moon is red.
The flowers in the fields are dead.
And the blood of Mang,
and the blood of Ming,
mingle in a thick-snake stream,
that writhing, burns to the sea
where the surge and pull
of deep-cut currents
scatter it, red, to every shore

for all the world to see.
The living nations hands,
with black-knit gloves,
clasp their bloodied eyes
and place their leaden skulls
between their useless thighs.
And when eternities have passed,
on some witless, arbitrary day,
the sun, returning full around,
casts a healing ray,
separates the two,
declares a fighting stay.
Mang, half dead, lies in blood.
Ming, half alive, crawls away.
Vivid in parting,
the memories of pain
are everlasting
and all in vain.

THROUGH THE PEARLY GATES
(Harold thinks about death and if there is life after death and he has a choice, he might like to consider what of this life he'd take with him, for death, undeniably, is a powerful part of the Acid Sea.)

If there is life after death, what would I take with me through the pearly gates? To answer that question would be to decide what is most important for me to keep and what it is I wish to shed. I would certainly like to have a healthy body, a bright spirit and an active mind. Though at times fraught with anguish, I would keep love. Its flower is beautiful and fragrant. I'd like to keep truth and beauty in all its forms; philosophy, science, art, music and a myriad of special preferences that I've acquired for a lifetime through my miraculous five senses. Most of all, I'd like to keep myself devoid of early destructive or negative extraneous programming.

I'd like to shed those parts of me that only seem like me, but are only attached to me and not me at all; illness, taxes, bills, dentist appointments, housework, etc. I must also be aware of what it is in me that is destructive, or extraneous that needs to be shed. This is difficult, for that which is attached to me often looks like me, and though attachments abound, they are often the most undetectable to one as close to me as me.

It is important I become aware of the destructive, extraneous parts of me and chuck them before entering the pearly gates. If I unknowingly take them with me, my heaven may turn out much like my life today and no better.

FOUR SYMBOLS

(Hal imagines the dove, a symbol of peace and love that is truly evident in the following poetic attempt. The dove perceives everything, hanging in space with wings as big as an entire continent. Omnipotent, he smiles broadly as he observes this beautiful planet with its life, death, windstorms, rainstorms, etc., and loves not only me, but all of life and death. Hal, tired of the Acid Sea, sees it as a happy description.)

> *One*
>> *Great white dove*
>> *hangs in space*
>> *wings as large*
>> *as East to West*
>> *smiles at me,*
>> *at life, at death,*
>> *loving all,*
>> *with every breath.*

However, things are not all good. Black crows symbols of censure, guilt, disapproval, and doing things against certain authorities, hurl words and epitaphs and criticisms against what should mean happiness.

> *Two*
>> *Black Crows*
>> *mock and jeer,*
>> *throw stones at me,*
>> *their yellow eyes,*
>> *swooping down,*
>> *call me names.*
>> *They glare and smirk*
>> *from the old dead tree.*

And the worsened part of me, burned to a shadow by my errors, sometimes not even knowing what they were, moves through life with all my equally erring friends who are also burdened with errors and mistakes and barely alive with guilt.

> *Three*
> *A charred stick figure*
> *hurtles through space,*
> *friend of the fire-wheel,*
> *holocaust victim,*
> *out of control.*
> *Solidified dread.*
> *Others follow,*
> *equally dead.*

As I grow, I expand. Maturity is gained. I grow and learn and investigate the past and reach conclusions, and each bit of knowledge that I gain helps to organize and order my life. I burrow deep and expand high and learn great knowledge and wisdom that nothing or no one can overturn and I live a wonderful life.

> *Four*
> *The tree, expanding,*
> *grows upward and out,*
> *filling the heavens*
> *with awareness and life.*
> *The roots below,*
> *grow downward and out,*
> *filling the earth*
> *with awareness and life.*

A WALK IN THE PARK

(Part of the Acid Sea of Reality is the minute by minute detail of my life as it moves through time. If I think about it, my person is continually in process through the fact that time moves unendingly forward in a straight line. In every second lies the opportunity for change, either willful or fateful, that could be miraculous or devastating. Consider being hit by a bolt of lightning from a distant cloud or the inheritance of a fortune from a forgotten relative. And so what follows is a detailed example of a minute-by-minute walk in the park with my wife and a few side stories upon which I free-associate that may leave you bored and anxious to return to your usual ways. Nevertheless, time is passing, minute by minute, and whether I like it or not, it IS a portion of The Acid Sea of Reality.)

Imagined conversation:
"Where'd you go??
"Walked in the park!"
"Yeah?"
"Yeah!"
"How was it?"
"Got a minute?"
"Yeah!"
"Well, it was Sunday morning and we decided to go for a walk in Malibu Creek State Park and went in the back way.""Yeah? Who's we?"
"Marge, my wife, and me."
"Where's the park?"
"At the Southeast corner of Mulholland Drive and Cornell Road."

It was noon and we locked our car under the beating rays of the midday sun that was baking the tired pioneer weeds that struggled limping and dusty on the road's shoulder. I slammed the car door shut after telling Marge where I was hiding my wallet - in the driver's side back seat door pocket. Why am I telling you this?

The walk starts a hundred yards south of Mulholland Drive on Cornell Road. From there, you walk east along a narrow paved driveway about a quarter of a mile through the southern part of a wide grassy field, baked brown by the summer sun and under a few ancient sycamores and poplars. They've stood there as huge, magnificent guardians of the wide yellow field and driveway for over a century.

It was exactly 12:11 PM, when, attired in walking clothes and running shoes, we made our initial turn off Cornell Road onto the slim, paved driveway. Marge, by the way, is a very patient and accepting person and not one at all to make a fuss. She's a fascinating, understanding person who seems to live a contented life letting be what will be.

It seemed important to mention the exact time we left on our walk in the park to be able to tell someone else, if they wondered what we did on that particular Sunday, how much time our walk took, or so that Marge and I could feel good about ourselves for having taken such an energetic walk, or if the walk turned out to be a short one, we just wouldn't think about it anymore, or mention it to anyone. But more correctly, I'd just finished reading an old treatment of mine, a short, cartoon-comedy starring Detective Fred and his buxom girlfriend Betsy, wherein Betsy had lost her pet cow - but that's another story. Detective Fred had a character much like Detective Friday in the good old television program, Dragnet. In fact

I stole the character from Jack Webb. He's dead now, so I presume, unless he's watching me from heaven or some other imaginary place, he won't mind. In the show, after knocking on the door of a housewife who appeared in a Kimono with horn-rimmed glasses and hair all over her eyes who seems compelled to keep talking and talking about something of no consequence was Friday's line, *"Facts, ma'am. Just the facts!"*

Be that as it may, we began walking down the State Park District's long, solitary, unpeopled driveway and we walked briskly because we had a lot of energy having eaten a breakfast of blueberry pancakes with slivered almonds, slathered in Marion's Marvelous Maple Syrup and a fried egg with orange juice.

At 12:17 we passed under the first giant poplar that towered and twisted dramatically into the sky with ancient authority. I could hardly make out the top, partly because I wear a baseball cap with a long bill with Yo-San University inscribed on the top. Yo-San is an acupuncture school that used to be in Santa Monica of which, my daughter, Viveka, is a graduate and now doing well in her own business for six years. But I digress! Anyway, it was difficult for me to raise my head high enough because of the effort to see way up to the top of the 100 foot tree and the sky's brightness was going to sort of smart my eyes. No birds up there, as I remember, but I did notice the wind gently fluttering the leaves at the very top before my neck began to hurt, then my back molars ached and I had to call it a day and give it up.

We marched along until we came to another of the guardians of the path, a tall Eucalyptus tree. It was exactly 12:21 and I noticed the black branches curling and twisting to the top and reminded Marge, not only of the exact time of today's discovery, but gave her information on why humans have an innate fear of falling. I'll bet you don't want to know, do you? In the Pleistocene age before humans were human, our ancestors, the more primitive man, made their way through the jungle tree-tops much like Tarzan of the Apes, except, of course, Johnny Weismuller used poorly disguised ropes upon which to swing, but in the olden days, the monkeys and chimpanzees and baboons were victims of prey on the ground, and so took to the trees to escape predators; lions and tigers and bears, tra la. Then, over millions of years and through eons of natural selection, they gradually acquired prehensile tails, grasping fingers and hand-like feet to catch the distant branches high in the air and move gracefully and naturally through the jungle treetops. Doing this was dangerous! If they missed a branch, they'd fall to their death, or at least break something when they hit the ground or at least get a nasty cut on the shin or be badly bruised on the noggin. That's why, as primates developed into humans, humans have a leftover fear of falling, a built-in prehistoric anxiety of missing the branch with ill-fated consequences. You see, part of us is still monkey! I'm not sure about loud noises, except if I heard a sudden ear-shattering sound, I'm sure my hair would stand on end, which is another archetypal reaction I won't go in to right now.

12:27: We arrive at two immense trees flanking the driveway! A breeze has picked up and is sweeping across the gently sloping, grassy, hot brown fields. The trees are poplar and I mentioned to Marge I'd always liked poplars, especially tall ones. This one, again, was at least a hundred feet high and its bright green leaves were wiggling and waggling in the warm, steady breeze to delight my particular eye, with one side of the leaves silvery, the other bright green. The congregation of leaves, as a large, cohesive family, were making a quiet, wind-driven whooshing. I mentioned to Marge that one huge branch of one of our neighbor's poplars had come crashing to the ground after a freak, lashing rainstorm. The wind and water teamed up to do the hellish work and overwhelmed the sturdy branch such that, with a violent crack and snap which I admit, I did not hear, fell thundering to the ground. Glen, our neighbor, had his men clean it up the next day. *"Out of sight out of mind!"* As goes the old saying. But on my 45 minute walks, which I take in the mornings five days a week, I still see that amputated broken part, high on the living tree, a memorial to what once was and shall never be again. That is, if I ever remember to look up there, which I probably won't. Ah, life! Ah, death! Was it ever thus?

12:32: We've reached several old fire department buildings that looked like one-story motels probably built in the 40s. They appeared strange and rather uninviting, except, perhaps, for emergencies of some kind. In addition to several cars and small trucks that appeared to be rusty and no longer working, there were a few nicer looking vehicles that might have been for the few employed who currently worked there. I assumed the buildings must be occupied because, though I saw no one there, I nevertheless understood that since the cars were there, that inhabitants were working diligently inside, probably on papers, or talking on the phone, or having a coffee break and personal discussions, or whatever. The assemblage of buildings and unoccupied cars seemed especially not to invite Sunday hikers. At least the quiet group that was probably inside the buildings was evidence of a place one might turn in case of emergencies, but that's neither here nor there, is it?

What I really want to talk about happened at precisely 12: 35. It was about an immense, free-standing metal roof supported by nothing more than 18 symmetrically spaced

6x6 posts and nine painted white trusses with knee-braces. The posts and trusses were on about 10 foot centers and the bottoms of the trusses must have been at least 16 feet high, which was also as high as the short eave. From the ground we could see right through and under the barely supported, apparently floating roof structure and even across the several acres of hot brown, grassy field clear to Mulholland Highway, wherein passed an occasional car or two with Sunday drivers on their way to grandmother's house or elsewhere. The floating roof had probably been an agricultural structure, possibly to shade cattle, or to provide shelter during delivery and birth of new farm animals; cows, goats, sheep, horses, etc. I called to Marge who was well ahead of me, *"Marge!"* She reluctantly stopped for she was well on her way toward the more serious, to her way of thinking, narrow dirt park pathway. *"Marge! Look here!"* Being an architect and familiar with wooden structures, I'd noticed no lateral bracing in the east-west direction on north or south side of the structure. I pointed out the posts that had no rigid frames in the east-west direction at either the top or bottom and that each free-standing post sat merely on commercially available concrete blocks. In fact, due to *"differential settlement"* of the earth, a term used by soils engineers to define the difference in soil to resist loads, the posts, and therefore the trusses and roof, had sagged in an arbitrary and inappropriate amount. I explained, not to a practiced ear, that buildings usually did not collapse vertically, but did, by wind or earthquake, collapse laterally, or sideways, to use a more understandable term. They didn't fall down, they fell over sideways because they couldn't resist the lateral forces of the wind or earthquakes. Isn't that interesting? You already knew?

12:38 I know you're thinking, *"Please, Ma'am, just*

the Facts!" Past the fire department buildings, the paved driveway ended in a turnaround, but I still wanted to see another old leaning structure *(God help us! Not again!);* A trellis doubling as a carport, under which was the relic of a car. The trellis had ancient paint-peeled beams and fascia surrounding the leaking, tar paper roof. What I thought was interesting was the span of 2x6 joists at 16 inches on center holding up flat, 1x6 roofing. I paced off a ten-foot joist span and felt relieved that my former house plans were OK! I'd just finished a deck where the spans were seven feet with a three-foot cantilever. They'd hold the loads. These had been spanning ten-feet for many years and were still in place. Marge waited patiently. Today, she said, she was not into buildings or time. I probably wasted three-and-a-half or four minutes with this personal sojourn, but joined her while subduing guilt.

12:42: We started down the gently sloping, narrow pathway between small weeds and tall grass about thirty-inches high. There was a small rise to the right with the beginnings of heavier brush and an occasional small tree. We marched leisurely; low vegetation caressing our legs.

12:45: Flowering mustard weed brushed my right thigh. We continued, Marge leading the way, myself behind following her pace, eyes on the narrow trail leading through the low brown, dry brush. I looked up now and then and smelled the light, warm breeze, and up and to the right to see heavier trees, and to the left across the acres of brown fields, the distant mountains, and I felt a sense of energy, peace, and contentment on this, our infrequent, semi-romantic, Sunday walking-through-the-park adventure.

12:49: Marge stops. *"Look! Pretty purple flowers with utter confidence radiating through the brown rye-grass!"* *"Yes!"* I reply. Then Marge starts off and I say, *"Here are more flowers. And by comparison, they're a different shade of purple, richer and deeper. Yours had more red in them."* No answer except the swoosh of our pants legs as they brush the dry grass and mustard weed each side of the path.

12:51: A fork in the path, one leading straight ahead through the brown fields, the other heading straight uphill to the right and to the recently seen heavier trees. We decided to take the somewhat well-worn pathway uphill and walk through the trees to keep cool in the shade.

12:56: We enter the woods. The trail is uphill and steep, but we assume it will flatten out once we're enclosed and surrounded by trees. Shadows cast patterns under the trees across the now slightly wider pathway and soon we enter into heavy shade and fluttering shadows. The path is dark, damp earth, which is quite a contrast from the bright and sunny pathway from which we'd just come. I was aware of more rocks and stones on the path and on both sides. In fact, I could look deeper into a kind of low woods consisting of live oaks, ceanothus, sumac, chamise and other stringy-trunked plants about which I know nothing. I followed Marge's steady footsteps, aware of the sound and pattern of the heels of her new Skechers walking shoes that have a convex instep that forces the foot to rock from heel to toe and is supposed to give excellent arch support. She says it is generally known that these rocker shoes with the convex arch improves one's posture, but I don't know.

1:05: In sudden bursts, our first skittering lizard zooms ahead of us. He seems to be curious as to what humans look like. He speeds ahead and looks, then speeds ahead again, finally zipping behind and to the side of a stone and doing a few push-ups. He seems unafraid but wary of these giant creatures that thunder along with massive steps that shake the ground. We're off to nowhere that he can think of. I suspect to him we are a fact of life that exists in the present and when we're gone we're no longer part of his world. With no knowledge of the past or future, his curiosity returns to zipping out of the tongue and ingesting any convenient bug or fly. *"Oh, to live only in the now! ... and Thou beside me singing in the wilderness - and wilderness is Paradise enow."* That's a quote from Omar Khayyam that goes like this, *"Here with a Loaf of Bread beneath the Bough, a Flask of Wine, a Book of Verse - and Thou Beside Me singing in the Wilderness - and Wilderness is Paradise enow."* That reminds me of a joke told by Bob Newhart. *"What if Caesar said, 'Friends, Romans, countrymen, I got somthin' I want to tell ya."* Wasn't that funny? Moving on.

1:16: The trail is steep. It's out of the sun, but continues relentlessly uphill. We hadn't bargained for this. My hips are feeling uncomfortable. I don't know if it's a touch of arthritis or side effects from forty-milligrams of a cholesterol pill I've been taking. There's no other solution. We can't go sideways, or up or down. We could go back, but it defeats the purpose of our walk in the park. We decide to tough it out and continue uphill.

1:21: Poison oak on the trail. Mustn't go there! The forest on the north side of the hill is thicker now, and there is lots of full shade and a minimum of the dappled kind. Wait! There's an open area under the shade of high trees and a picnic table! Wow! A picnic table way out here in the wilderness! Marge heads for it and sits down and crosses her legs. She takes out some nuts on which to nibble. We catch our breath. Marge has to wipe the dust from the picnic bench. I, if course, being male, don't need to do this. I just sit right down on the bench, dust and all. That's what males do. We don't do laundry, right? We rest and continue our walk. Ugh! More uphill, this time a little downhill to a minor dry creek, then again up a steep shaded trail. We climb and climb. Soon it's getting sunnier. We're reaching the top.

1:29: The trail stops against a barbed wire fence! How could somebody do this to us? We find a way around the fence by an ancient path covered with weeds, some yellow daisies, and more purple flowers and find a deep cavity into which we would have fallen had it not been for the barbed wire. I immediately forgave the person who put it there and instead, blessed him. He kept us from perhaps falling over head-first into a bed of poison oak and with great difficulty in removing ourselves with possible scratches, bruises or other injury.

1:32: Aha! We've reached the top. We can now look over the wooded crest to see the valley and distant mountains toward the ocean and to the south across the valley of Malibu Creek State Park. It's sensational! We're standing in heavy weeds and it's still sensational! We look for the path to descend. It's not well marked, but more of a bunny trail. The only other direction is back the way we came or away from our desired destination by means of an equally poor trail heading north. We decide to descend in a southerly direction on the less attended bunny trail going, evidently, more quickly and steeply into the valley of Malibu Creek. We slip and fall and twist and turn and wind and loop and stagger and stall and do everything we can to not fall and break a hip and, perhaps, be rescued by helicopter. Actually, If we did fall, the descent is so steep, our upper body would not fall far, because caught in heavy weeds, we'd not be hurt. When we are close to the bottom the footing has turned to loose, dry shale, crumbly and slippery on a steep slope. The trail looked designed to facilitate easy falls. I fantasize one of us falling and breaking one thing or another, but Marge and I both make it. We congratulate ourselves and vow never to take that trail again. I said to Marge, *"This is an impossible trail. There must be a better way. This is the way a trail looks when it's never been used. Even bunnies find another way!"* She heartily agreed.

1:37: Finally, with sore feet, we're at the bottom. We've mastered the impossible trail, but we feel mastered by it! We quickly find the main trail leading to and from the entrance parking lot. The intersection is perhaps a half-mile from the main entrance to the park on Malibu Road and a good two miles from the end of the trail and off into the tuilleries - that is, there are so many trails all over Malibu Creek State Park, to use a hackneyed phrase, *"it would make your blood run cold."* My blood is running cold right now. How's yours? We head back toward the entrance and nearer the small pond fed by a creek from which Malibu Creek State Park gets its name. That would be the Malibu Creek State *Pond*. Other walkers are turning into the place from which we just came. There seems to be a wider trail much lower than the one we and the bunnies descended. I warned the hikers not to take THAT trail, pointing to the bunny trail. They followed my pointed finger but did not hesitate to walk toward the wider trail. I thought to myself, that's the trail we should have taken if we would've been smart. I said to the hikers, *"That other trail is the IMPOSSIBLE TRAIL!"* They avoided my gaze and looked at me as if I were dangerous and continued their journey rather hurriedly up the wider path.

1:41: We walked east along the main wide trail. Young people strolled to and fro in singles or couples. Two middle-aged people inquired of us if we knew where adventurers climbed and repelled off cliffs. I said, *"Yes! You've just passed it. Follow the same trail back along the way you've just come and when you get over that rise, follow it down the hill and bear to the right along the base of the hill for a quarter-mile or so following the creek. You'll find it, because the way you go in is the only way you can go out."* They thanked me, did a u-ey, and in the same way in which we were going, quickly outdistanced us because we were walking so slowly and tired because of taking the slippery downhill, impossible bunny trail.

1:46: We circled to the right along the creek passing couples now and then, going this way and that, until we arrived at the pond just this side of the Malibu Creek dam. Among other surrounding trees, a low willow tree was swooping over the land and water. It provided a good place to sit. I urged Marge to sit with me while I took off my Adidas and socks to cool my feet. Boy! Did it feel good. Marge took this resting time to enjoy the peaceful surroundings. There were high willows around the bottom of the slope and strong oaks along the hillside. Birds gave their chirps and occasionally sang their plaintive songs and the water was calm and reflected the vegetation and mountainous side opposite the pond. A couple and their kids were having lunch at a picnic table. What looked like a broken raft sat pulled up on the shore with no one attending. A couple of guys and an attractive young lady were in the shade of an oak, whispering, a few people came, saw and went. Marge, sitting on the tree trunk beside me, broke out a few nuts for herself and we shared a small plastic container of applesauce. Marge has the beginnings of diabetes and watches what she eats and drinks often and carefully. She has to take blood samples and the recent knowledge of her affliction has cramped her style, but she continues her life rather stoically despite her somewhat disturbing diabetic condition.

1:51: *"Just the facts, Ma'am!"* I know you'd like to say. It was time to get back, we'd been gone by my stopwatch exactly an hour and forty minutes. I put on my socks and shoes, being careful to wipe the dust off my feet, however there wasn't much dust because the earth under the sloping willow trunk was semi-muddy and so it is more proper to say I brushed damp mud from my feet, except there wasn't much mud, either, so there wasn't either dust or mud, but I was mindful about checking. Mother or Marge would say, *"That's a good boy!"*

We walked back along the way we came until we got to the intersection where there was an Andy Gump into which, we both were pleased to relieve ourselves. Then we returned along the way we came and I thought that I had not seen any of my favorite beetles that rather purposefully and confidently cross the path. Actually, having looked it up on the internet, my favorite is called the darkling beetle of the genus *Eleodes*. It has fused wing covers and cannot fly. Since the beetle and I are a couple of my more preferred living creatures, I guess this is my favorite beetle. Out for a walk on early mornings five days a week, I've noticed the darkling beetle likes hot, sunny days. Perhaps that's why southern California is its favorite home. There's another type of *Eleodes* that in an alarm situation will stand on its head and at those times has been known to emit a foul odor from its rear. It's called a stink beetle, or more commonly, a stink bug, so, since I can rarely tell the difference between the two, I guess my favorite beetle sometimes is, I'll have to admit, called a STINK BUG!

1:55: Marge and I continue walking pleasantly and silently, hand in hand, our thoughts, if any, to ourselves, enjoying the mountains, the park the flowers, the path, and nodding to trudging couples or families or single hikers going in the opposite direction. My stink bug thoughts led me to thinking that I had not seen any tiny little frogs near the pond. In June around the Rocky Oaks Park pond near our rural home can be found hundreds of tiny frogs. Why not Malibu Creek State Park pond? I have to admire little frogs. I feel a kinship toward them. We each share this part of our planet in our own way in that together at this particular time in all of universal history we inhabit the edge of this very same pond. They hop all over the path and the path is sometimes far from the pond. I wonder how on earth they got here on this path so far from their birth place. They're only 3/8 of an inch long and a 1/4 of an inch wide. Legs fully extended, they'd have trouble reaching three quarters of an inch. Nature has also endowed them with camouflaging colors; mottled light and dark brown on their top-sides and warm, off-white tummies. While marching along, I can hardly distinguish them from a pebble for when not moving they look alike. I have to slow down and watch carefully to pick my way through the tiny frogs. I see them sometimes five or six at a time, hopping left or right, this way or that, to escape my thundering tennis shoes that could quickly crush them. They must regard me as an impossible foe. They do not know that, like a God, I'm watching over them. Many times I've found them, in lesser numbers, far from the edge of the pond. I know the pond is the place of their birth, since I've seen them as tadpoles. I wonder how the little frogs, so tiny as they are, make their way to a path through thirty, forty, to fifty and sixty feet of tangled, rye grass, climbers, vines, ferns, parasites and wildflowers. If I imagine myself as this tiny little being, and considering my finest leap to be less than an inch high, and no farther than two inches, how under God's magnificent grace, could I ever hope to maneuver my way through such a terrifying jungle of giant weeds. I guess, with their pliable bodies and flexible extremities they wiggle this way and that, climb over miniscule leaves, fall miniscule depths and with a relentlessness and the driven power of their young and natural instincts, they make their impossible way wherever they're going. We'll leave it there.

2:01: Tucked back into the mountain about ten yards, we've reached the intersection of the bunny trail we came down and the main Malibu Creek State Park pathway which is a pathway to everything else, like creek crossings, massive stones, the *M*A*S*H* television show site, hills and valleys. I remember this spot, since it's the only *"T"* to the north on the main path and is marked by a four-by-four post four feet high which I now notice has vertical lettering saying *"Gates Creek"*. I surmise it was discovered by a fellow named Gates. We turned and saw again the trail we came down. Another couple walked in with us and I said, *"Don't take that funny looking trail. I call it "THE IMPOSSIBLE TRAIL."* They looked me over, but did not acknowledge my warning and passed ahead of us in doubt and as if to ask, *"What's he talkin' about?"* I noticed they were headed toward another, wider, better, more traveled trail, obviously the one Marge and I should have used to come down. A couple of middle aged hikers emerged from the same, wider trail and I asked them, *"Does this go through to a flat plain of dry brown grass and Cornell Road?"* They said, *"We're not sure, we came in from the other direction, but we did notice a continuing pathway going west."* That was all the information Marge and I needed to know. We thanked them and began climbing the wider, shadier path under oak trees, poison oak, toyons, sumac, chamise and the normal California natural vegetation next to a rocky barranca Gates or somebody else called Gate's Creek.

2:09: The wider, less steep path was much better and the going was much easier. We went at Marge's pace, Marge leading the way, which was slow and steady. We were making good time, I thought, when suddenly, during a steeper part of the climb, Marge sat down on a large rock. *"What's wrong, Marge?"* I said. She was breathing silently but heavily and after a pause, she said, *"I'm short of breath."* I felt alarmed, though I didn't want to overreact. We waited for her to catch her breath. Soon we were on our way again, Marge leading the way, again walking slowly and steadily.

2:13: We reached the flat plateau, a further extension of the original broad flat, gently sloping acres of warm, brown weeds and rye grass with Mulholland Drive and a few Sunday drivers in the distance. I recognized where we were. All that was necessary was to follow the single file path west a mile through the brown, tall grass and mustard weed to our car on Cornell Road. This time we decided NOT to take the shady, path, the beginning of which was uphill from our present location, but walk steadily and purposefully to our car. We moved silently, Doug following Marge, on a trail so narrow it would not permit side-by-side walking. Though the land was more or less level, still it flowed gently up and down and we sort of rolled along through the dry, grassy plain. Though I was tired, I was not exhausted. I don't know how Marge felt.

2:17 After another ten minutes, Marge had to stop again, standing and leaning over with her hands on her knees to once again catch her breath. *"Everything all right, Marge?"* I asked, *"Just resting a little."* She replied. We continued walking, Marge first, Doug second, at a slow but steady pace. When we were within sight of the fire department buildings, I said I'd move ahead at a swifter pace and get the car and drive it back along the slim paved road beneath the tall poplars to the fire department buildings so that Marge wouldn't have to walk the half-mile distance of the paved road. She agreed, and I set off to swiftly walk the paved road and get the car. I didn't jog, because, though I go three miles, five days a week, I walk, because jogging makes my hips hurt. So I walked briskly up a gently sloping hill to the paved road and was surprised at how far it was from the brown plane of dried grass even to the paved safety of the fire department buildings. While walking, I worried that Marge might have another session, however severe, while she continued walking and I was getting the car.

2:22: I walked past the fire department buildings, the heavy metal-roofed former agricultural building, beneath which still sat a few tired vehicles forever shaded in eternal relief. Then the immense guardian trees, standing stalwart into eternity, and just before reaching Cornell Road, taking a shortcut across a large circular gravel parking lot and a hundred yards of plowed fields with grasses and weeds to leap over a low, white wooden fence to the car. Quickly starting it, I made a U-turn on Cornell Road and entered the slim, paved drive and drove swiftly back to get Marge. I was delighted to see her walking on the paved road and was thrilled she had made it past the heavy-roofed agricultural building. She was advancing slowly and steadily, as is her manner, toward the car. I was elated and my feeling toward her was one of love and admiration for her reasonableness and courage under conflict and her steadiness and inner strength and undemonstrative will power. She got in the car. I turned it around and we sailed out of Malibu Creek State Park toward home. It was 2:26. Our adventure took us exactly two hours and fifteen minutes.

(Epilogue: That was the end of our park adventure. At home, Marge said she'd been dehydrated and should've brought along water. I was worried about her need to rest and shortness of breath. I wondered if it was symptomatic of her diabetes. She said it was. What we learned was that she must have food and water to take with her at all times and that I needed to know what to do should any future emergency situation arise. Other than that, we had a marvelous time, but so far nobody has asked us what we did or how long we were gone on that wonderful June Sunday when we went on a walk in the park, but at least, if you read this, we are overjoyed that you know.)

THE ANSWER
(Harold has the Answer book.)

I have a book called <u>The Answer</u>,
but I never read it.
It lies on my desk in the corner.
It gathers dust.
The jacket curls.
I long to know what's in it,
but I have never once reached for it.
At night, sometimes I cannot sleep.
My head spins.
I try to think things out.
I am thoroughly at loss.
(Straws on the wind,
leaves on the tide.)
The answer book lies,
inert,
on the corner of my desk,
lent by a well-meaning friend.
Its cover bears the title,
<u>The Answer.</u>
It will explain everything, fine,
that I need to know.
And I desperately need to know.
When I complain,
as I usually do,
my friend says,
"Please open the book."
<u>The Answer.</u>
I always plan to.
I "plan" to right now.
When the mood strikes me right.
When the stars are aligned in a beautiful design.

When the moon whispers to me during an eclipse.
When night winds promise rain
on the 5th of December.
I do have the answer in my personal possession.
It's in that book, there by the door,
The Answer,
all of it written
what I'm going to know.
I have never reached for it.
At times I do not think I see it.
Perhaps I don't want
my friend's answer.
His may be dull.
What if mine were
a rampageous river,
begging to be followed,
up the frigid canyons,
in the hollows of the turns,
through the mountains
and the meadows,
bright with flowers.
The answer book's a thief,
robs me of discovery.
I must learn not to ask
for what I don't want to know.

COMPLEX AND COMPLICATED
(Well there is a little to be said about complications and complexities. Perhaps complexities can be interesting, but who's to be the judge? Harold would like an uncomplicated, harmonious life. What is his house like and is there a relation between his house and himself? I think so!)

Now, it has been on my mind to write a little about the difference between the words, complexity and complicated. We all think we know the difference, but there is a point where complexities, of a sudden, turn into something complicated. To study that line is the purpose of this essay.

As an architect, I will take the design of a house as an example. A good house, one that is boilerplate, because it has all the earmarks of utility and harmony in a pleasing background without complication, and is one perfectly suited for any family life.

The walls will be of one thing, let's say off-white drywall on the interior and off-white stucco on the exterior. The entire roof will be the same, let's say asphalt shingles, the exposed ceiling, natural, unstained wood or drywall. The cabinet work and doors will all be of the same wood, let's say oak, as well as the countertops all being the same, let's say, same pattern Caesarstone, throughout.

The floors will be the same, for instance, quarry tile inside, but slipping easily outside to the adjacent patio. Throw carpets may be used for those times when bare feet want to be warm. The sculptural quality of the entire house would be powerful and correct with good lines, fine forms, plenty of light with harmonious colors, set among trees, patios, trellises and foliage for a delightful indoor-outdoor feel. The entirety testifying to a useful piece of artwork that gets out of the way, while being a delight to the eye for those with places to go and things to do.

If the couple wants to sit down with a glass of wine on their chaise lounges and see where they live, their home appears together and magnificent.

Such is the story of a well-designed house. But, you say, how is the particular personality of the owner expressed? Any particular personality must be worked out within the mind of the owner, but certainly it should not be in something that brings disharmony to the final structure.

For argument's sake, let's say a husband or wife decides to change the countertop in the bathroom to express her individualism and personal liking.

Well, the solidity and harmony of the house might be strong enough to take it, because the bulk of the building meets all the rest of the requirements for good design. Changing a countertop might be called a *"complexity."*

But, then, if another member of the family wants an oak floor in his room and another wants carpet in her room, then the artistic value of the entire structure is further compromised. The complexities have increased.

Perhaps one of the kids wants a blue room and another wants a pink room. Now a harmonious house is down on its knees begging for forgiveness.

At this point the integrity of the structure is no longer a point of issue. The house has lost its artfulness, its composition, its harmony, its honesty, and it's *"what you see is what you get"* personality, its *"reason for being."* We've made a horse into a cow in that it has been overly compromised. It's gone! The house, though it still may function adequately, has now lost its harmony and the perpetrators have crossed the line to complicated. Is a person similar? Can't we be uncomplicated while still being a work of art?

MY NOTHING

(In the larger scheme of things, Harold knows he's not special, but on the other hand, he's grateful for what he has, and is, in another sense, special.)

I shall proclaim it to the hills,
sing it to the flowers in the fields,
shout it to the multitudes
that gather in the streets.
It shall be heard,
my nothing.

For I <u>will</u> have it heard.
I shall cry it to the gull
that hovers on the wind,
and to the stalwart trees.
(I'll bring them to their knees.)
I'll bring my message softly
to the violets in bloom
that arch their dainty heads
to escape the forest gloom.
I'll whisper it to frogs and snails.
(Tie a message to their tails.)
They'll know the tale that I must tell,
my nothing.

And when the winter winds
come whistling through the fields,
come crying through the backyards
and open country fields,
and then the sloping snowdrifts
and crisp and crystal night
comes settling on the surface
on some special starlit night,

I'll stand alone and think,
project my message strong and clear
so all the universe will hear it,
(to me it's very dear)
my nothing.

DRIFTING OF CONTINENTS

(Well, what does the drifting of continents have to do with Harold and the Acid Sea of Reality? If one is to experience life, any intelligent creature such as humans have the ability to learn about past history and to project their speculations (which sometimes don't mean a thing) into the future. No other animal in the entire earth's existence, except humans, can or could do this. Is this a miracle? Harold uses his speculative mind!)

Well, continents don't exactly drift; they are more or less continually pushed out of position by molten lava oozing up between long oceanic cracks. Lava under water spews out along a two-thousand-mile fissure, solidifies, and during long arbitrary time periods does it again and again and again, etc., forcing the earth's crust ever outward. It's been doing that for over four-and-a-half billion years. All that lava leakage ought to move something! It does! It crowds the underwater earth's crust made of water, mountains, plains and canyons against similar above-water mountains, plains and canyons, with such force more mountains along the striking plane are formed. The heat generated is so strong, volcanoes blow up, scattering molten rock along the immense *"Ring of Fire"* and earthen magma shoots into the earth's air, spreading vital minerals throughout the atmosphere. Or, it may erupt more slowly, spewing brilliant, boiling, hot goop that flows down the slopes *(think the big island of Hawaii)* to harden in the water or cool to earth temperature. Doesn't that make you want to hear the kick of old Buddha's gong?

The idea of continents being pushed continually and what would seem arbitrarily out of place over earth's lifetime is a heady thought, indeed. Where do we go from here? Well! All present living things die, of course, geologically speaking, in a very short time, but the earth will continue its customary rotation, be pulled this way and that by the moon, heated by a slowly-increasing-in-size-and-warming sun *(the sun swells and heats as it dies),* pursue its cosmic fate and be subject to its continuing normal erosion and eon-damage occurring during its approximately nine-billion-year lifetime.

What will future earth be like? I suspect oceans and land will continue to exist and here and there life will repeat itself as it's done in the past. Miracles, as now, *(think the colorful and wondrously shaped creatures of the coral reefs)* will continue into the future.

Archetypal living forms, like sharks and turtles and birds and insects and the famed duck-billed platypus may continue to live longer than those less adapted to a longer life, but as the world turns, life will generate from microscopic to immense living creatures and everything in between. Life will be of all shapes, sizes and colors and an understanding creature will be blown away by the inconceivable complexities of an older future planet, if, at that time, there is such a future understanding creature.

THE CROW
(Harold is convincing in this symbolic poem
clearly about his scolding parent.)

The crow on the fence post
 sits, convinced.
He flaps and stretches,
 and assumes a pose
 of tense repose.
The sun is hot.
The crow, more so,
 because he's black.
His yellow eyes
 burrow deep
 into all he sees.
His expression, mean,
 behind his beak,
 unrelenting.
I wonder when he'll fly away.
He stays, it seems,
 for hours,
 watching, waiting,
 cocking his head,
 burrowing his eyes,
 staring, searching,
 observing.
Nothing escapes him.
What he doesn't see
 with his eyes,
 he feels through the quills
 of his feathers.
His essence is everywhere.
He permeates the atmosphere.
He stands, the center

of his own aura
of sensitivity
and meanness,
and I, the object,
must "cotton up"
or receive the big,
    "Or else!"
He sees in me
something vile
I see not within myself.
He does not see
    how beautiful I am.

THE EXACT DIMENSIONS OF HEAVEN

(Harold has just finished a book called Life after Life, a treatise by George Anderson, one who sees images of the deceased. Anderson says, "There seems to be a kind of consciousness that exists for each of the dead." Harold believes him because there seems no reason for untruth. And Anderson isn't able to paint a specific picture about what life is like after life, and he cannot sufficiently describe heaven or tell us what it's like to be there, but Harold wonders if people just make it up.)

There are classical tales, like the vision of Hell in Dante's book, *The Inferno*, and we get a visual look at Heaven and God by viewing Michelangelo's classic Sistine Chapel ceiling artwork. God, in human image touches his creation, man, with his finger, giving him life. He is attended by angels. Unhappily in this picture, he didn't give this gift to woman. You all know the idea of heaven with Gabriel and his horn, the pearly gates, celestial music, divinities with wings, and the picture of all deceased humanity enjoying singing the Messiah and the Hallelujah Chorus. Is this some idea about the hereafter?

But now, with modern science and new developments in astronomy with computers and laser beams and wide-screen television sets, high-tech celestial receivers and satellites orbiting the earth, older images of life-after-life seem implausible. Isn't it time to update our thinking?

For one thing, man, other than his miraculous brain, is not so different from higher animals. Man and chimpanzees and elephants and goats all have a head, two eyes, two nostrils, two ears, four appendages, one head and similar insides and means of procreation.

Through evolution, all creatures derive their present form from lesser species and may even be a preliminary form for their advanced species. I personally think the Great Unknowable shaped every animate and inanimate thing. All have elements of God, even if some are parasites *(like us)* whose existence depends on other life.

AIDS takes over our cells and destroys our immune system and we die. Did the Unknowable make the AIDS virus? Yes! For what reason? I don't know. Perhaps to reverse evolution. Why? I don't know, but the Tyrannosaurus lived for 135,000,000 years and it's been gone for 65,000,000. Evolution backfired, or died. Lizards lived off lizards. Now they don't. There are questions.

Of course, all the inanimate material, water, earth, rocks, stars, moons, planets, the sun, gaseous nebulae, quasars, are all part of the great Unknowable, too. I believe when a man or animal or plant, or any other living thing, dies, it becomes part of the inanimate material. Everything is either animate or inanimate. However, for a while, during the act of decomposition, energy is given over to make other animate things. For example, if your cat dies of old age and you bury him under a tree, worms, larvae and bacteria form partly from the decomposition of his body. The remaining chemicals, vitamins, minerals, carbon dioxide, etc., furnish food for the tree.

One thing dies and in decomposing gives life, as if the energy of a living thing is used to give life to something else; is reused for more life. Then when its new life-giving substance is exhausted or washed away or used up in further growth or blown to the ends of the earth, the former living thing eventually becomes wholly inanimate. But it becomes the dwelling place of the animate. It's only a theory, but without inanimate water, we have no animate fish, without inanimate mountains we have no animate mountain goat.

A curious question; without fish, who would sense the

water and without animals, who would breathe the air, climb the mountains and sense the earth? To get back to George Anderson's experience, we can say that as humans when we are alive we have consciousness and when we are dead we either have or don't have consciousness. I like consciousness when I'm feeling well. I get an unconscious feeling when I'm in the undreaming, deep sleep state. In this state I could remain for a few minutes or eternity and would never know the difference. I'd have no sense of time. For me unconsciousness is timelessness, time being important only if I am aware it is going by.

In the unaware state or in the deep, undreaming state, there is no fear, no thrill, no hardship, no growth, no creation or procreation, no thought, no feeling. If death is an unaware state, I'd rather be alive, aware and in good health.

If there is a chance of death, and I'm certain there's a good chance, I'm going to search the universe for evidence to take me back to the living state. Sometimes, I hope this so much that I don't care what living state I come back to; lion, elephant, mouse, fish, bird, lizard or another living creature. I might like to come back as a plant, given no other choice. This is called reincarnation.

Of course, I would prefer to come back as myself; give myself another try. If I could come back once, perhaps I could come back twice; in fact many times. Just be reborn time after time; perhaps forever; have eternal life.

Belief is defined by David Viscott as *"knowing something is so, whether or not it is."* There are many instances when I may need to believe something so strongly, it's as if I were an abused child yearning for unconditional love from an unaware parent. Can God be substituted for the unaware parent?

It's intrinsic to life that it wants to continue. I have

talked about awareness and unawareness, life and death, on and off, black and white, true or false. But what about the third alternative, something neither living nor dead, neither aware nor unaware, something like George Anderson's visions? George talks of seeing images of the deceased hovering around a living friend or relative. They speak to him symbolically and sometimes verbally. He has no clear idea what their life on the other side might be like. They seem to have died with unfinished business to be conveyed to the living and then recede into the unimagined, undimensioned, place of Heaven.

The exact dimensions of heaven are difficult to imagine. In fact, it is difficult for me to imagine the life of any other living creature. For instance, I have no idea what the life of a great white shark might be like being able to detect an electric impulse a thousand times weaker under water than I can detect. I can't imagine living the life of a hummingbird, or a grub worm, or life as part of the plant world, or a microscopic parasite in the eye of a fish. Indeed, it is just as difficult to imagine the life of fellow creatures, as it is to imagine, or be sure of the existence of life after death. Of course, I can at least observe the life of other living things.

Without denying someone might know of the existence of life after death, I would say I have no clear picture in my mind or feeling of what this after-state is like. If I try to invent it, might I not project my own hopes, fears, desires or feeling into the story? I personally don't trust another's knowledge more than my own.

David Viscott defines knowing as *"the truth from a certain perspective,"* and it seems we all have different perspectives.

A perspective coming from science or philosophy is that the closer we get to that solid stuff of which the world is apparently made, the more that stuff disappears; becomes like waves or undulations or vibrations in various frequencies. Matter sometimes approaches the variety of wave signs like those found in music, so the existence of both living and non-living stuff, that is, the entire universe of which we are a part, can be defined as a glorious symphony. We, living and non-living, may be beautiful music. A wonderful thought.

But is the parasite content in the eye of a particular and unhappy fish, part of the beautiful symphony? Perhaps the music is not continuously wonderful. Think of Somalia, Bangladesh, Argentinean jails, and pollution, diminishing flora and fauna, acid rain, ISIS wars, the severe population explosion. Perhaps the unhappy situations lend guts to the music. Sometimes the music is arduous, sometimes lyrical. Discords may be necessary for the life of a dramatic symphony; keep it from being continuously too beautiful. Most good music has an edge to keep it from becoming too pat. Are Somalia and AIDS and pollution the edge to our planet's symphony? Will the edge kill us? Where will we go?

Again considering George Anderson's special talent, whether after death a conscious entity floats around learning things, or whether there is an interim between multiple lives, or what conscious entities do while they're in the intermediate state, whether they like it or don't, whether they have chores to do or are in a state of continual euphoria, or in limbo-land, or assigned to living creatures as their guardians, or there is clothing or nudity or decorum or shame, whether there is a best and, therefore, a worst is really only conjecture, isn't it? Perhaps the best and worst are necessary for our own planet being our own heaven.

Knowing is *"the truth from a certain perspective."* One point I feel strongly but openly about is that if all living creatures, cells, plants, people, etc., die, that is become non-living, it is unreasonable, in my mind why ants, tics, bananas, roses, armadillos, monkeys, penguins, people, snakes and toads could not be admitted to the interim state; *neither living nor non-living.* Unless, of course, someone made a rule such as, *"only those living creatures who can reason, remember past events, and plan for the future and can invent marvelous machines, can be admitted to the transition state."*

I don't know whose been inside the head of a bug lately, but it is possible, in ways of which I have no knowledge, they make things for their own survival, invent music and have an instinct for past and present equivalent in wonder to our own reasoning power.

I say, the truth from a *(my)* certain perspective, is that if humans, who by the way, are the most destructive creature ever to inhabit the planet in recorded history and who are destroying it through overpopulation, overuse of resources, and pollution, are entitled to the new, astral plane, I would have to think all other living things, every bit and always part of the living music, are also entitled to move into the new astral plane.

Perhaps they are waiting their turn on the reincarnation ladder as some would believe. If all these creatures moved on to the interim astral plane and considering the horrendous number of living creatures since life began a half-billion years ago, the plateaus of heaven, given the natural habits of all living things, must be packed solid with creature spirits. In fact, deceased life over there might be much like our living world. Who can really say?

So now I have made a cloudy picture of the living and non-living, the conscious and the unconscious and now the third possibility, the interim plane, neither alive nor dead. At this time, then, I wish to embark on my own specialized *"exact dimensions of heaven,"* a view of that mysterious in-between of living and non-living things. Of course, I will have to make it up.

LOMBARD

(Harold remembers the first six years of his childhood, a lasting part of his Acid Sea of Reality.)

I remember Lombard
And sporadic lightning
Flashing in the east
And the humid hush
Before the rain.
And then
A crashing bolt
That strikes the line
Runs down the pole
And with a blast and flash,
Strikes the main.
Soft rains falling.
The Mulberry trees.
The Elm in back.
I sleep by the window.
Droplets strike my face.
My only pair of chaps.
My picture taken
When I was six
Missing two front teeth,
And myself with Marshall
Digging in the field.

ABOUT DEATH

(Hal thinks about death. Why not, he's in his middle eighties. Many of his close friends have died. It's age-appropriate for him to think about death. In fact, thinking about death forces him to be more aware of this miracle of life. Isn't it true, life on earth is also life in heaven?)

The French female writer, George Sand *(1804-1876)*, speaking of her former atheist tutor about to die, heard him ... *"fervently uphold the authority of the church...he had been unable to accept the horror of nothingness."* The words, *"horror of nothingness"* symbolize the tutor's idea of ceasing to live as his awareness of the depressing loss of life as a miracle!

I don't fear after-death, because unless there's heaven I'll no longer have awareness. I will not think, feel, see, hear, or have strange feelings something's odd. When the five gorgeous senses are kaput, there <u>is</u> no awareness.

I do fear being uncomfortable before I die. Before my pacemaker, I almost fainted at the computer. My irregular heart decided to pause for three or four seconds and blood didn't get to my brain. Things went black and I slumped over in an almost faint. They called it *"syncope" (transient loss of consciousness).* If the heart can stop for so short a time almost causing death, what fragile creatures we must be. I knew that dying because of a heart stoppage is a piece of cake. I faint, become unconscious, and while I'm unconscious, I die. No strain, no gain, no pain! How simple is that?

Of course there's the reverse of the story. Long ago, my former wife had cancer of the lungs and brain. She struggled with physical and mental agonies for over a year. In the last stages, increased morphine produced a coma-like existence and it became useless in stopping pain. After a long and disheartening fight, she was forced to give up and allow fate to continue its hideous unroll.

Then there is the story of a her father who, after seven long years in the Veteran's Hospital, eventually died of Alzheimer's disease. The bedridden years were difficult for the living and the pleasures of life for the victim were zero. But how am I to judge the value of life to a person so victimized? I can only assume. I don't fear death. I fear a painful death.

Then there was the story about a person given devastating news;

Doctor: *"You only have twelve weeks to live."*

Patient: *"Will I be in pain?"*

Doctor: *"No. You'll function normally for eleven weeks but the last week you'll be in enormous pain."*

Patient: *"Can't I skip the last week?"*

My mother avowed euthanasia years before she died at almost ninety-four. She'd expressed herself previously in a newspaper article showing there are times when a widow has lived a good life, i.e. childhood, young adulthood, marriage, family, children, retirement, and old age, and has grown to a stage of being physically and emotionally tired; bowels not working, catheter-fitted, each day demanding courage and perseverance, pain and unhappiness. She should at least have a choice. Mother, a strong person otherwise, outlived her desire for life four years before she actually died. My brother and I were pleased when she finally and naturally obtained her wish.

My father died while defecating. One early morning my mother heard a sharp cry from the bathroom. Hurrying, she discovered my father on the floor in front of the toilet. She called her son, Dave, who gave his Dad a half-hour of artificial respiration before the paramedics arrived and took him to the hospital where he was pronounced dead from a massive heart attack. No autopsy was performed and no further investigation seemed necessary. We miss him, but all things considered, and as dying generally goes, Dad had a pleasant death. Am I wrong?

There are infinite stories of death from terminal diseases, starvation, plane crashes, tsunamis, tornadoes, hurricanes, earthquakes, fires, wars, etc. There are as many deaths as fingerprints and each individual, human, plant or animal, will experience death in a different way.

Which leads me to believe that we have all been given birth by a single mother; the earth. The earth is everything's mother and we are brothers and sisters of earth's family. The earth, with its sun, moon, water, slim layer of air and thin, permeable crust, is the medium upon which we live and the plain facts are that an unimaginable number of the planet's former living beings are now dead. In fact they're still here. They make up part of our earth's crust. *(In a single tick of the cosmic clock, I'm strata.)* They may be part of our topsoil and we may be walking on them.

Interestingly, dying is a singular event, since each of us dies in our own particular way. No one can die for us. We each do it alone. Thinking about death begs the question of the meaning of life and who cares anyway. First of all, the deceased don't care, because they can't. We have to excuse them.

Does the universe care? What about the grand scale of our universe? The universe, with its Big Bang 13-1/2 billion years ago, black holes at the centers of galaxies, the irrevocable speed of light, the actions of gravity, the powerful electromagnetic force, the protons and neutrons held together by six quarks and the strong force, and the impossible-to-imagine concept of space-time. Let's face it, in the last analysis, our miraculous universe doesn't care. Only we, living, intelligent living beings who are so miraculously smart that we can examine ourselves and ask why, have the outstanding ability to appreciate ourselves and the wonders that surround us, are the only ones who care.

I care about those I love. I might even say, we, as humans, care about those we love. Loving and caring go together. I understand that everything of which I'm aware are miraculous and I value miracles. I care. Humans care. Humans intrinsically understand they are miracles and consequently value and appreciate themselves as such.

In conclusion: The universe doesn't care whether we live or die. Whether the universe cares or not is meaningless. Humans and everything on this planet are what is meaningful because we are the best part of the universe's meaning. While our life or death is meaningless to the universe, it's meaningful to every living thing on this planet and expresses the miracle of our existence as a whole.

I can visualize the universe as the father and the earth as our mother. I am a child of the earth within the context of the universe, the father. But, for all practical purposes, neither the universe nor the earth will mourn my death. All I have is the heaven I find while I'm alive on earth. I assume I speak for everyone when I say I value my life as meaningful to me and I care.

ONE TASK FINISHED
(We all have our tasks to finish. Harold's task is not much different from all humans on this miraculous journey.)

I have finished what I set out to do.
It has been seven months since I started my task.
Occasionally my work went swiftly
as it does when I play or do what I like.
At other times the minutes seemed like hours
and the hours seemed like days.
The paragraphs I have spoken.
The paragraphs I have written,
*   I cannot count or remember.*
The gestures I have used
and facial expressions used
to get across an idea, meaning, or feeling,
*   I cannot count or remember.*
The breakfasts, lunches, dinners I have consumed,
the clinking of eating utensils,
the clean clothes I have soiled and washed,
cannot be counted or remembered.
And tales I have told to my wife and children,
and attitudes, either happy or sad,
or tired or hostile, or humorous,
and the attitudes I have evoked
or provoked in my family
*   cannot be counted or remembered.*
The examples I have set, either good or bad,
the energy that has passed through me and was
*   used by me*
from sleep to food to action to excrement,
the animals and plants I have caused to die
by my need for them,
the foliage, fungus, bacteria,

that now live solely because of me
cannot be counted or remembered.
The dawns, the arching of the daily sun,
the sunsets that have set, the moon chasing Venus
or Venus chasing moon and the myriad starlit
      positions
with respect to each other during the time
of my seven month task,
and the changes in the political atmosphere in this
      country,
and in all the countries of the world,
and the births of babies, and the deaths of the
      elderly,
and those fighting for their lives in hospitals,
or in countries that have insufficient food,
      cannot be counted or remembered.
And the murders and heroic acts in saving people
or animals, or on the sea or natural countryside,
the rainstorms, the droughts, the hurricanes,
snowstorms, blizzards, cyclones, fogs, sleet, white-
      outs, calms,
that have occurred, while I was completing my
task are impossible to total.
The minute erosion of all mountain ranges
and hills, the minute increase in ocean salinity
resulting from salt in streams rambling into the
sea,
      my own irrevocable aging,
the minute deepening of lines in my face,
and the deepening of lines in the faces of others,
the minute maturing of my own and others
personalities,
      cannot be counted or remembered.
All these things and infinitely more,

took place while I was completing my task.
And though at times, it was difficult,
I'm glad I completed it.

STOPPED WORLD
*(A dream interrupted Harold's introspective
contemplation and he understood there was a difference
between stopping the world and being alive in a world
that's stopped. In the Acid Sea, such an epiphany can
occur. Such is a continued advancement into that vast
realm of personal ignorance. Or is it just maturity?)*

At four in the morning, I dreamt I'm in a classroom figuring
out the lyrics for a song. It's a choral piece and I can't get it
right. I've written three extensive paragraphs of verses on
a blackboard at the side of the classroom and am deeply
lost in thought. I've studied the piece and it's still not right.

It's possible the class has been helping me. While I'm
standing, chalk in hand, I'm aware of a gray-haired person
sitting to my left. *(Marge has gray hair – it's probably
Marge.)* One hand to chin, the chalk hand dangling, I was
thinking things had continued with normal sounds and
sights when of a sudden everything is stopped; frozen
in place. I glanced at Marge, her head motionless while
slightly turning; the clock, the sun, moon, clouds, water,
trees, and universe were in place, stuck, solid. I panic,
understanding something deep and cry out. I toss, turn
and try to escape and become relieved when I awake.

Heart racing , I am glad to be in real life and out of the
dream. I lay in bed, the back of my hand on my forehead,
staring at the ceiling. God be praised, Marge is still sleeping
by my side. I'm glad to be living and thinking in the world
again and I layed still to consider the dream.

If you've watched a DVD that had suddenly stopped
with the characters fixed in time and place, you'll
understand how the dream looked. In that situation, of
course, you can take the disk out, wash it and replay it, or
fast forward past the scratch, or return it to the store for a

new one. You're not in a real place, immobile and frozen and can deal with it. It's just a malfunction of the disk.

But what was so devastating and what I understood in the dream was the terror of being an alive, thinking, feeling person, while the world, so to speak, had *"died with its eyes open."* I remember only the back of Marge's gray head, stationary and immobile. Before, she was mindful and aware, but now immobile and poured in place like so much cement. I could walk around her as if she were stone; gone, as if dead. An unusually bright light accentuated the room's stillness. If the clock had been ticking, it had stopped, as well as its hands. My few assumed classmates were calcified in their chairs.

Evidently, the dream was my organism trying to internalize the sudden death of my son-in-law's father. He'd not told anyone of his cancerous and terminal illness, had refused treatment, and surprised everyone by his sudden demise. This affected me deeply. But, in the dream, why did I panic? Because of the loss of that which I take for granted and assume is the normal part of my life – an undying and eternal movement of the world.

*There's a difference between stopping the world
and being in a world that's stopped.*

I'd known the idea of stopping oneself in the world, but how would it be if I were the only one to move and the world were suddenly stopped; the sea, frozen like blue plastic ice unable to wash ashore and ineffective in giving the soft swish of waves on sand? If the world stopped, whales and sharks would be trapped in moving positions, apparently dead in the arbitrary depths of ocean. No breezes would rattle the leaves on a tree and the birds, having been stopped in flight with wings outstretched, motionless in the air. Clouds, like pieces of cotton, stuck on the face of a bright blue unfeeling sky. The sun, immobilized and bright, a rigid ball in the air, unable to rise or set, like some lifeless picture. It would never be night unless I walked to the other side of the world, but, now, I'd never see stars, the moon, the Milky Way, Jupiter, the Southern Cross. They'd be lost in the bright, unfeeling midday. Friends would be frozen in the positions of places to go, things to do, unable to budge or speak. Cars and trucks stopped on the way. There'd be no one alive with which to share my wonder, thoughts, amazement and I'd wander this lifelike, stationary zoo 'til food gave out with only the loss of everything I held dear; abandonment and hell on earth.

STOPPING THE WORLD

In one of Carlos Castaneda's books, he has a chapter entitled, *Stopping the World.* This is amazingly different than being alive in a world that's stopped. *Stopping the World* actually means stopping oneself while the world goes by. To practice *"stopping"* he advises going to a remote place, sitting perfectly still for a long period, perhaps a day and night and being aware of all that occurs. I imagine myself sitting in a meditative way, perhaps in the Lotus position, alert and sensitive to all occurrences.

One morning years ago, as an afterthought, I found myself trying this. I hiked to the top of Gorilla-head, a low mountain ridge that parallels the ocean several miles inland that stops suddenly before falling steeply several hundred feet into Bonsall Canyon. From the rocky promontory, I was able to see the Pacific Ocean with a faint shadow of Santa Barbara Island on the horizon, the tops of oaks and sycamores deep in the valley directly below, and hills and valleys eventually rolling off to a hot inland desert.

Mildly tired from the climb and not due anywhere, I found a patch of dirt in a narrow clearing facing away from the ocean where I could clearly see inland toward the bulk of the continent's land mass. Low native brush was to each side and I sat with legs forward and arms behind and for a short time, relaxed. I looked over the rolling hills with thick brush that made up the green valley and distant peaks. The sun, almost overhead, was a bit behind me. A few fair-weather clouds dotted the sky. The temperature was comfortable and I thought I'd enjoy a few minutes.

An oblivious bug came out of the brush and strode purposefully across the clearing as if it, also, had somewhere to go and something to do. It hobbled over pebbles, around twigs, before vanishing in the shadowy foliage on the left. I loved the bug with such audacity, or perhaps, purposeful unawareness is a better terminology.

A slight breeze cooled my face and as it did so, rigid stems and leaves, stiffly moved back and forth before becoming still again as the breeze died. I remained observant and noted the low brush, perhaps not over two feet high, had stronger leaf shapes and colors than a different variety of brush below. The taller dominated the smaller below. It became obvious, a competition was going on. The more established plant was in control and enjoying a big life to the fullest. It dominated the smaller weaker plant that was in the shadow and that reached outward for sunlight, fog and a share of moisture.

There were twigs lying on the ground in different shapes. They faced this way and that, lying parallel or crossing one another in strange patterns. Some extended or disappeared into the brush. Some lay comfortably over small rocks, an end resting on smooth soil. Rocks had *shadows*! A strange dark line beneath and to one side of the rock was its shadow. Shadows of leaves, twigs, the whole bush, my own shadow, shadows that leaves & twigs cast on other leaves & twigs, and all changing slowly as the sun moved its imperceptible way.

Then ants. How could I not notice ants? Perfectly in my view a few feet away was a low mound of ant debris, like a heap of coffee grounds, in the center of which was the darkness of a quarter-inch hole. Now and then an ant would emerge, and at more or less regular intervals, another would descend. Yes! There was a vague line leading to or from the hole with ants going in opposite directions, touching noses, facing this way, getting lost, facing that way, always continuing, full of controlled energy and relentless.

The clouds were in a different place! They'd changed shape and had drifted slowly and silently to the west. Tiny clouds I hadn't seen, appeared. Clouds that were there, mysteriously evaporated. The sky was alive, living and dying with clouds. A single engine plane high in the sky, oblivious to that below, droned briefly by, flew over a mountain and was gone. A red-tailed hawk appeared from nowhere, made wide circles deep in the canyon and below the horizon without flapping its wings. It soared with aerodynamic turns silently riding the updraft and was soon lost over the hill.

I didn't follow Carlos' rules about stopping the world by staying all day and all night, but I got the idea. The world was alive with movement. All I needed to do was stop so that I could see it. I remained where I was for forty-five minutes which is pretty good for a get-up-and-go kind of guy. When I'm still, the things of the earth are violently in motion. In fact, things of the earth are always violently alive and in motion whether I observe them as so or not. It's because we exceed the speed limit in our cars, or are late for appointments, or have to meet someone for lunch, that we don't notice the quiet but violent activity of the whole world around us.

Had I remained all day, the shadows would have

reversed their positions following the pattern of the sun. The ants, as the earth's automatons, would have dug deeper holes and built higher piles. The clouds would have thickened or gone away according to wind, temperature, or moisture.

Had I stayed all day and viewed the ocean, Santa Barbara Island might have faded and given way, as on another day, to a dark, cloudy front quickly approaching from the west. It would have steadily, moved across Point Dume and covered the bright bay with a shadow of dark, midnight blue through which were formed intensely bright patches of light from God's grace that would have appeared on this magnificent surface. Godlike rays would stream from openings in the clouds.

If I'd stayed the night, I might have seen the sun bursting its way through a thin strip of clouds in the west over the water, or the moon rise and the temperature drop. I would have seen stars appearing, Venus reigning first, then the Milky Way bright and fading near the horizon, or the fog on a cool breeze, advancing swiftly and silently and obliterating sound and sight, hiding the path leading me home.

To me, this is a lovely story. It makes me happy to know the world is passionately alive whether I am or not. It gives me a sense of peace, even if I were not here to enjoy it. The world persists forever. Somehow, I live again because I'm of the earth and, dead or alive, will be of the earth. I've seen it in most of its glory, I'm a part and shall in whatever form remain a part.

You see,
*There's a difference between stopping the world
and being in a world that's stopped.*

LONG TAIL STREAMING

(Of course Harold wants the best out of life. He wants to fly and soar, not be bounded in mud and unable to move. Here he imagines how he wants to feel while riding on a cloud-driven, watery, mountainous, miraculous earth.)

For the first time
That tornado
Came howling,
Rushing,
Tumbling into my heart
Attending its space.
For a while
It had me spinning
Like round petals
Of a native bush.
And I saw the sparkling horizon
An instant before
I leapt into the wind.
And rocketed skyward,
Long tail streaming.
I rode the freshness
Of cold air
With tingly skin.
And from the center
The swirling clouds
Claimed their space,
Expanding,
Billowing,
Rising throughout
With the richening colors
Of stratospheric blueness.
Until that special star,
In bluish darkness

And the sharpness,
The brittleness,
Until the flashing pinpoint
Of that very special star
Binding all together,
Becomes the catalyst,
The essence,
The object,
To which there is only
Flowing toward.
And I,
Feeling the miracle
Of the ages,
Soar with it,
Long tail streaming.

ON BELIEF
(It's easy for Harold to have simple beliefs, but later
he seems to drive it into the wall. Is there any
excuse for him?)

I believe the sun will come up tomorrow because I've lived for over eighty years and during that time I've been there in the morning while day after day it always came up.

One time our dance group hiked to the top of Bony Ridge Mountain and we sat among the morning grasses and watched the sun silently creep above the horizon. It was a magnificent and simple proof of the sun's excellent track record. It's been doing that consistently for 4-1/2 billion years and I'm just as sure as the passage of time that in the morning the sun will come up.

The moon, too! All my life I've observed the moon going through its normal phases, high in the night sky, zero to crescent to quarter to half to three-quarters and finishing with a glorious, outstanding full moon, illuminating windblown wheat fields and tumbled crags of broken tree trunks. In the full moon's night, animals roam the darkness to feed. Snakes slither for food, purposefully as in a dream. Hoot owls begin at 4:30 AM and mountain lions with yellow eyes prowl for nocturnal prey. I believe, yes, the moon will rise.

I believe in rainstorms, snowstorms, sleet, fog, clouds, wind, hurricanes, tornadoes, and dust storms because I've either experienced them or seen them on TV.

I believe in DVD's because I can watch television and I believe in transportation systems and computers because I have driven to Staples to get and use one.

I believe in ocean pollution, diminishing sharks, shellfish, and barrier reefs, air destruction, clear-cutting of forests, lessening oil reserves, melting icebergs, wars, starvation, genocide, poverty, exploitation, extinction of human and animal species; selfishness, greed, mammon, and lack of compassion for all living things with what seems an almost complete human disregard for our only habitat.

I believe in do-gooder organizations, too, like the Red Cross, Salvation Army, Goodwill Industries, Sierra Club, Cystic Fibrosis Foundation, Habitat, Feed the Children, American Cancer Society, Meals on Wheels, Aid to American Veterans, and those individuals and groups who have compassion for the increasingly pathetic condition of our miraculous world.

It's easy to believe in things in front of your nose, but what about the concept of God, ambivalence toward organized religions, arguments for and against abortion, the paranormal, natural evolution, politics, and life after death?

I believe in a universal force some may call God that allowed all that of which we are aware and all that of which we are not aware to exist.

Imagine the Big Bang; beginning at a point so heavy that tiny scientists call it *"the singularity,"* and then an explosion so immense as to have created the universe and everything of which I know and don't know. All this within an immense empty space that's so huge, dimensions can only be measured in relative distances between physical bodies that are continually expanding.

Now, if you will, draw an imaginary line around the whole universe and notice our galaxy is wherever you'd like it to be and our planet is within that galaxy; the whole inside the drawn circle. Notice, too, that we are on our planet and this forces me to know I am a small extension of the Big Bang, or *"Star stuff!"* As Carl Sagan would call it. I am part of the Big Bang whether I choose to be or not!

I'm also on the planet whether or not I choose.

Everything is the ultimate result of the Big Bang and I choose to call it the universal force. You may call it God or something else, but what results is a universal force of which I and all plants, animals and minerals are a part.

Parallel lines, like railroad tracks, never meet. I have to accept that fact. Cutting things in half to find the smallest building block of the universe continues over and over until all that's left is another smallest block to divide. I have to accept that fact.

I can always add one to the largest number I'm capable of imagining and I have to accept that, too.

If God, great in his purpose, designed the Big Bang, I'd have to ask who made that God and who made the second God, and third, ad infinitum, until all that's left is only another question, who made that one? I have to accept that fact, too.

Parallel lines that eventually meet, or the division of things resulting in an indivisible singular block, or discovering the one and only final God is unreasonable. I have to accept that fact.

It is reasonable to believe that some things in my universe have no finite solutions. Some things are unsolvable. That's also a fact.

What is, is! And, pardon me if I repeat, I have to accept that fact as well.

I bought a refrigerator and was told the light goes out when I closed the door. Imagining no other way to test the on-off state of the light, how would I really test whether the light went out when I closed the door?

I took a chair and sat so that I could get my face down real close to look at the edge of the refrigerator door and closed it watching very carefully with my keen eyesight and was unable to see if it really went out when the door clicked shut. I came away with no closure; no assurance that I was not wasting electricity. I wasn't sure whether it went out or not, and no sign of relief that I'd really know whether the light went out or not. Of course, the example is ridiculous, because no intelligent person would design a refrigerator light to stay on while the door was closed. I believe that, too, but how could I be sure?

If my life were the glowing light with the door open and I illuminated the refrigerator contents, myself and the surrounding kitchen cabinets and floor, and closing the door was death and the man told me the light *(my life)* was supposed to stay on while the refrigerator door was closed and even glow brighter when the door closed, how could I be sure?

Those who've had near-death experiences are convinced there is life after death; however, they were still alive however close to death when they came to know that truth. They weren't dead like the raccoon I saw one morning lying, lifeless in its own dried blood, dead as road kill on the highway. It remained there for a few months before it quietly disappeared and blew away.

When people like my mother and father have passed beyond to unequivocal death, how do I know they're living a brighter life in the hereafter? I don't, and that's a fact I have to accept, too.

What then is this *"through eternity"* everyone talks about? There is no eternity except the large, small, or medium changes that any particular person left, minimally or maximally, upon our present day world. Thank you, Edison. Thank you, Ford Motor Cars, thank you, Mark Twain, thank you, Shakespeare, thank you, Beethoven.

The condition is similar to parallel lines that never meet, the division of matter resulting in yet something to divide, and being assured that one deity is the absolute and final God that made everything. Like the refrigerator light that is supposed to go out when the door is closed, I can never really know and I have to accept that fact.

Serious praying is profound hope that calls out for help to all known and unknown sources of aid.

Praying my child recovers from a severe illness, or that I don't get killed or injured in the war, or that my leaking boat stays afloat until I reach shore and I've done everything I can to correct the situations, are serious prayers. Prayer is the ultimate hope that something I've missed, universal or local, in this wide, wide universe will come out of the blue in time to give me the help I request. It's a desperation act and that's a fact.

For all serious problems, I would pray to beneficial forces for my recovery, such as doctors, nurses, high-end equipment, family and others willing to aid, that make up the helpful portion of the miraculous universal force. If I call the universal force, God, I would be praying to God. It's essential I *"keep my powder dry."* Prayer is making it known I need help. It's possible I may never know the source of what aids me, but the more signals I send, the more help I may get. The more I appeal to those who are willing to help, the better. More loving brains are better than fewer loving brains. Perhaps, advertising in desperation is the way to go!

There's a difference between reasonable and unreasonable praying. If team members are unhealthy, unmotivated and unpracticed, reasonable praying degenerates into wishful thinking. To win the big game, forces have to be in place and team members must be healthy, motivated, practiced and working in harmony. Wishful thinking is not praying. To me, to determine the difference between wishful thinking and praying is the point.

FATE

(Fate is so much in evidence while Harold deals with the Acid sea of Reality. In fact fate is the most important element anyone has to deal with in the Acid Sea. He has to think it over.)

Why should I wish to live if I must contend with
  ever-present Fate?
For life cannot be lived without impersonal,
  non-caring,
  non-living fate.
I can choose not to live,
  or choose to live,
  side by side with fate.
I was in a state of non-living before I was born.
  I know what non-living is about.
  I am unconscious when I sleep.
But the alive state allows me to be conscious
  of humor, joy, love,
  sadness, pain,
  indifference, enthusiasm, etc.
Alive, my cup can be seen as
  half-full
  or half-empty.
I can give fate its power,
  but I can keep my own.
Fate is impersonal,
  does harm as well as good,
  is unaware,
  often appears arbitrary,
  and undependable.
If I give Fate its power and keep my own,
are we then to be adversaries?
No! Because

Fate is not a living being.
   Fate is not a <u>someone</u>.
Fate has no feeling.
Fate does not judge.
Fate has no human characteristics.
   Fate just IS!
Fate can lift me to freedom,
   or leave me worse than dead,
   or manipulate me anywhere between.
   Fate is not someone who dislikes me.
Fate is not someone against me.
Fate is not someone who cares
   or does not care.
Fate is dead to feeling.
Fate is lifeless and inanimate,
   though, at times
   it can work for good or bad
   through the living.
Fate has hills and valleys.
   To clamber laboriously upward
   or slide gloriously downward.
A person can <u>use</u> Fate.
   <u>I</u> can use Fate.
I can use Fate to my own gain.
   I can slant Fate to my advantage.
I can be opportunistic.
   I cannot hurt Fate
because Fate is <u>not</u> a living being
   and cannot be hurt.
I may choose to injure living beings,
   but to do so,
   I'd injure myself.
But I may do anything I want with fate
   and not feel guilty,

because Fate is incapable of caring.
How can I use fate to my own advantage
    while not injuring others?
That is the question!
    I have power.
My power derives its strength from possession
    of mind, body and soul.
I must eat proper food,
    get sufficient exercise,
    sleep regular intervals,
    have a love life.
The remainder of time I may <u>use</u> fate
    to my own advantage
    to improve quality of life.
What is the quality of life I'd like to improve?
    If I'm functioning without pain,
    what do I want to do with my life?
If I can manipulate fate to my advantage,
    if I have mind-body-soul and power,
    how can I use fate for my own gain,
    and what do I wish to gain?
Being alive, that is,
    accepting ever-present fate,
    allows me to
    fulfill my highest purpose,
    bloom my biggest bloom,
    develop as the uncaring
    indifferent and unsympathetic Fate allows.
Who knows, I may get lucky.

(Enamored of pursuing awareness, Harold, whose creative spirit is not convinced of life after death, is curious to understand the imaginings of those who are. He envisions how three long-ago departed humans are now fulfilling eternity with their otherworldly time. Love is always the bottom line.)

My name is Ensa and I'm known as the Lady of the Clouds. I have chosen your planet, Earth, as my special observational object. My colleagues refer to me as the *Earthen* Lady of the Clouds, for there are many Ladies as well as Gentlemen of the Clouds observing the vast numbers of cloud-filled planets throughout the universe. In this discrete solar system on the edge of this equally discreet galaxy, my special friends are:

> *Burkir,* the Jupitarian Gentleman of the Clouds,
> *Anka,* the Saturnian Lady of the Clouds, and
> *Lufa,* the Venusian Lady of the Clouds.

Millions of years before your planet was born, I and my special friends and immeasurable others ceased to exist. On Earth, you'd say we lived our allotted time and died. When we died, our spirits were swept into the realm of the after-death experience, the eternal habitat of the spirit's afterlife. Among enormous selections, certain of us made choices to monitor, study, and enjoy one or more of the incalculable planets throughout the universe. Unseen, we chose to travel and live in the clouds of our chosen planet and observe and record its processes as a history of the universe eternally being prepared for newcomers throughout universal time. Your planet, Earth, was my choice and I've been observing it since the first stellar dusts and gasses combined to form the flaming core and cooler life through its future dissolution in eight or so billions of years.

My male friend, Burkir, studies Jupiter and lives unseen, courageously riding the Jupitarian clouds. They consist mostly of dense hydrogen, but have substantial quantities of helium, water and nitrogen. Powerful winds are dominant in the crossing jet streams that are home to hurricane-like storms; one of which creates the Great Red Spot whose radius is over eight-thousand miles, well over twice the radius of Earth. Within the violent current of chemical air are brilliant, continuous and repeated explosions of lightning that are seen as dimmed for Burkir because of the heavy atmosphere. They've existed for over three hundred million years, and I've got to hand it to Burkir, for the fortitude and superior adrenalin he needs to ride these raging storms. He often hurtles deeply into the center of the furious planet, there to witness the smallish core of molten rock.

My female friend, Anko, rides the entire planet of Saturn whose outer rings are made of millions of ice particles whirling endlessly around the main Saturnian world. Some hurtling chunks are small as a grain of sand and some as large as a tumbling car. Saturn is called the ringed planet. Space separates each ring from the other and for organization here on Earth are given letters for names, A, B, C, D, etc. Ring F, and I presume the other rings as well, are shepherded in place by two moons, Prometheus and Pandora. Anko, like a powerful horsewoman, rides and navigates the ceaseless rings, sweeping before and aft and monitoring Saturn's eighteen moons. She investigates with enthusiasm and delight Saturn's atmospheric history and is curious about its future. Since Saturn is a gas planet, its atmosphere is much like Jupiter with swirling storms and lightning flashes interminably occurring throughout its life of billions of years. Anko tells me her experiences are every bit as exciting as mine and as passionate as Burkir's.

Lufa traverses and observes Venus, the hottest and brightest planet in your solar system. It's sometimes called the morning star and about the same size as your Earth, but covered with impenetrable clouds that are compounds of carbon dioxide and sulfur. It curiously spins west to east, opposite of your Earth, and its temperature exceeds 464 degrees Centigrade, or 867 degrees Fahrenheit. Invisible, Lufa withstands the temperature conditions as we all do of our chosen planet and enjoys the inexorable evolution in the eternal passing of universal time.

Though my friends are particularly happy in their choices of violently interesting planets, I feel I've made the best choice. Your Earth is over two-thirds water and is placed at the exact and proper distance from the sun to prevent waters freezing or evaporation. It has a thin layer of oxygenated, warm atmosphere with gases and proper materials to sustain life. Having lived, myself, over eight billion years in the hereafter, I know that planets with these conditions are rare and that few other planets are so arbitrarily and happily positioned from their mother sun.

You cannot see me, but I live within the clouds. Over the full eight billion years of the planet's life I continually encircle the Earth, and like an observational aircraft, I'm aware of Earthen happenings every minute of every hour of every day. I don't need to sleep and in the cool mornings enjoy investigating and jotting notes on your world as I quietly descend with the fog and infuse your atmosphere, or when its late at night and I've drifted off the lake into the trees and have, so to speak, captured the atmosphere, I beg you to stop, look, and be aware, for I am the fog, and loving it. I need you to feel special when you remember that airborne moisture is an incredible gift and that it doesn't happen on the majority of planets throughout the universe.

When a black cold front moves swiftly over the desert and flashes of lightning spear the ground and you are enthused by the promise of rain, know I'm there from that most violent of vantage points, watching and loving you. Or above 26,000 feet when I and the clouds shape flimsy mare's tails with their occasional falling ice crystals called *"virga"* that evaporate high in the air, never reaching the ground, know I'm joyful in my life and happy in my place. Or when I come twisting like a tornado or whirling like a hurricane, remember, this is your blessed planet and do what needs to be done to preserve it and admire it for it is a miraculous atmospheric condition that's so rare as to exist on barely any other place.

I've enjoyed my four-and-a-half-billion-year stay with you and you should know it's been a wonderful experience. Your recent two thousand years amounts to the thickness of paint atop the Empire State Building and is a miniscule, meaningless episode in the planet's total life, but for me, and I wish it for you as well, it's been a lovely, fascinating experience. Advances in creativity, intelligence, and the practical uses of each have grown at an exponential rate. Positive organizations do their best to slow global warming, some providing non-polluting power, saving oceans and forests, conserving fresh water, intelligently harvesting food, decreasing animal and fish extinctions and acting to slow overpopulation. Though many problems still need to be overcome in your short inhabitation of this wonderful planet, the heavenly fathers and mothers have put forth that this planet Earth shall move through every special crisis and continue to exist its pre-arranged eight billion years of allotted time without exception.

I, Ensa, will be with you as long as there are water and clouds on your Earthen planet, for I am called The Lady of the Clouds. The founding fathers have decreed that everything that lives, must die, so when the Earth is relieved of its clouds and is a cold, dark mass, my job will be finished. Don't worry about me. I'm immortal! Since I live throughout eternity and there is no such thing as the end, I'll turn in my report so all new arrivals may instantly know of its every feature, trilobites through dinosaurs through mammals to humans. I'm sure they'll make associations and build on this new information, because that's what the afterlife is all about; learning, progressing, knowing, feeling, recording, and being creative, but most of all, the act of loving. You are loved, Earth, and our wishes are for all living creatures to understand and enjoy a special unrepeatable period of your eventual and eternal lives and to love to your heart's content.

DREAM STORY

(A writer friend of Harold's asks, "Have you nothing to tell us at all? Can't you think of anything to write that would involve the reader so powerfully he would forget his own person and "become the book," so to speak?")

I'm not sure I have that ability.

I'm not sure it's fair of me to ask you. I know you are doing your best. But what else can you tell me?

I could tell you about the Elm tree in our back yard.

No! I don't want any more Elm tree stories!

We had an Elm tree in our back yard. I'd secure myself with a clothes line to the topmost branches and doze and listen to leaves in the summer wind.

Please, no more tree stories.

Eventually, the sun lowering and a cool breeze blowing would make me chilly and I'd untie the clothesline and make my way down.

Is that the Elm tree story?

I'd have impressions of the tree and rope marks on my thigh and arm.

I'm getting tired. Let's forget the past for a moment. What are some of your present day philosophies?

I've been thinking on my own existence lately.

Oh boy! Existentialism. I just love Sartre.

I'm not exactly Jean Paul Sartre.

I didn't mean to compare you. What have you been thinking lately?

It's more dreaming.

Well, what have you been dreaming?

At the time I'm dreaming I don't know I'm dreaming. I think it's really happening to me.

Go on! I won't interrupt you. I like dream stories.

OK! I recall this place I've been before. It doesn't seem

quite real. I recognize the poorly-constructed house still cantilevering over the water's edge and I recognize the foreboding gray ocean with heavy seas I feel are lying in wait for me beyond the mist. I must enter the house. It seemed a child I knew must be in there. Such a rickety old place, and the ocean surge is given to striking it, running along the sides, the structure feeling the push and then the pull of the backwash tugging at the creaking walls, coaxing it into the gray water.

Sounds kind of spooky.

Yes.

Sorry.

I felt strange there . . . as if I'd been there before. It was much smaller than I'd remembered . . . Just one room, really . . . with one small window, elbow high, and looking into the gray bleakness. I looked out the window. I didn't like looking out the window. The sea was grim and threatening. I couldn't be sure what was lurking beyond the mist. Some giant wave, no doubt, to do me in. It was my fear this ancient, crippled building would break off and I'd be swept with it out to sea, beyond the mist where it would sink, slowly, disappear silently into the gray depths and I'd perish, alone.

This is more like it.

Then, the peak of the high tide was happening. That one most mighty breaker of the highest tide, an immense wave swept by the open door taking the cracked wooden steps with it and loosening the structure from its foundation. I think, when it returns, it will surely carry us out to sea. If I jump out the door, I'll enter the rushing gray water and risk being carried into the wild surf, alone. It is better to stay where I am. Here comes the back surge. The flimsy shed is jarring from its foundations. I am being swept with it into the gray, heaving water toward the obscuring mist.

Uh! Huh!

The experience was not as frightening as I had expected, the house was broken from the sandy beach and I had been carried with it beyond the surf. The loose room with me inside was being buffeted by high seas and chop. It was not floating level, but was reasonably dry. The cold mist permeated the room and I was splashed, now and again, by saltwater through the glassless window. It was not sinking, I thought. It was not coming apart – at least, not yet. It is by no means a sturdy craft nor a bulwark against the elements, but seems pliable and is holding up. As I waken, I come to the terrifying realization that the ship of my life is at full steam and mother is not at the wheel!

Mother is not at the wheel?

That's right. Mother is not at the wheel!

I don't get that part. What does that mean, "mother is not at the wheel"?

I take it to mean that I have finally understood that many of the actions of my life were to please mom instead of myself and that she, as an elderly person, doesn't care what I, as a mature man, does or does not do in life and I must begin acting to please myself.

Holy cow! This is too heavy, man. People don't want to hear about your problems. That dream stuff was OK, but this philosophy stuff?

You said you liked existentialism.

I do, but, do you think it will sell?

Sartre did OK.

Yeah! But you're no Sartre.

That's true.

I think I preferred the elm tree stories.

ACCOMMODATION

(Accommodation is similar to tolerance because it requires thinking of others, or in this case other inanimate objects. Accommodation is a universal concept whether between the animate or inanimate that fosters harmony. Harold needs to know this because, as he says, he's a sensitive guy and thinks accommodation, tolerance, forgiveness, and understanding are necessities.)

Noel and Chava were building a steel trellis over our concrete patio outside our too-small house and Noel asked me if I wanted the 4 inch square steel beam end-tapered to match the roof slope or cut square. I should have already decided, but he caught me vacillating because the idea had never occurred to me. Thanks, Noel. I'm fond of telling clients, *"You can't miss what you don't know."* I didn't know whether to cut it square or tapered because I hadn't considered the choice. I hadn't thought about what was possible and, therefore, couldn't miss it. *(Out of sight, out of mind!)* Now with the question in my head, I had to deal with it.

I'm a sensitive guy. In one of my cartoons I show a comical mid-life man lying on his back under a tree while a dead leaf flutters down towards his body. I called it *Anxiety Buildup.* The man now has to deal with the leaf; either forced to roll over out of the way, perhaps on new, cold grass, or brush it off as it lands on him, or catch it with his hand and toss it away. The fluttering leaf created in the ultra-sensitive man an anxiety buildup because the thing, without the man's thought, volition or desire, and seemingly out of context *(a fate thing)*, decided at this particular moment to detach itself from the motherly branch and fall on him! It demanded attention! Who called for that?

I decided the beam-end should be tapered to *ACCOMMODATE* the roof. Why must the roof be accommodated? Because it was there first and it's bigger; kind of like a respected elder or meeting an already famous personage. I imagined the roof being introduced to the accommodating beam-end and being pleased at the friendly gesture; that it was being cut to match the roof, eliciting a rousing, *"How nice!"* In my crazy imagination, I imagined the house smiled at the considerate cut. The beam was pleased to accommodate the slope because this was its gift to the too-small house. Motivation to give is one of the great benefits from God or the universal forces and always allows me to feel good, which is the most important emotion to have in life.

The beam-end was cut on a matching slope to accommodate the roof allowing the new steel trellis to work in concert with the too-small house. It acted in a friendly, cooperating manner in consideration of the elder.

Were the steel beam cut straight, it would have remained, for some undisclosed reason, aloof and self-centered. There would have been no gift, no accommodation, no compromise, no consideration for the established presence of the older house. The too-small house might have felt rebuffed and taken offense at being so ungraciously ignored. It might even have been considered a not so minor tiff. The straight-cut beam would not have availed itself of the opportunity to show caring for the too-small house. Instead of being considerate, it would have remained standing by itself, alone and cold with few friends seemingly to have its way.

When parts suffer, the whole suffers. The assembly would not have been as complete, integral and powerful as it could have been with the beam unaccommodating. The house and trellises' ultimate capacity, would have been diminished, if ever so slightly.

The architect's job, or my own job in life, is to envision a delightful whole that can be or could have been achieved. I must dream the completed whole with mindfulness, intelligence, integrity and beauty so that those not so creatively inclined will at least know what they can have, or could have had, so they'll have it, or if impossible to know it, regret it, and be able to miss it. Architectural elements and all humanity must work together in a spirit of ACCOMMODATION to create something better for the whole. *(Am I wrong?)*

HAPPY BIRTHDAY ME!

Happy birthday, foot!
Walked on any water lately?
Happy birthday, arm!
Waved any good-byes, today?
Any hello's?
Happy birthday, brains!
Had any good thoughts
with which to occupy yourself?
This is the 30,660th
day of our life.
What a glorious day
to be alive, folks!
One of the best I've ever had.
I still see pretty well,
and hear pretty well,
and the rest of my senses
haven't suffered much
for being almost
31,000 days old.
Happy birthday, self!
You've done a good job
just living this long.
I sure am proud of you,
and wish you
6,000 more
beautiful days of life,
even better
than the last 30,666.
Happy birthday, me!

EPIPHANY

(It seems Harold has an epiphany. What's that? An essential perception or insight into the reality or essential meaning of something, usually initiated by some simple, homely or commonplace occurrence or experience.)

Rodale's Synonym Finder describes the word *"epiphany"* as a revelation, insight, realization, awareness or understanding.

It also expresses knowledge, which is derived from the word *"know,"* in ways too numerous to list. They all have to do with being cognizant or conscious of, or to be enlightened. When I use the word knowledge or know, this is the expression I mean.

I had an epiphany this year. I understood the fine line between opposites. This revelation was such that I should capitalize the epiphany and say I had a realization of the fine line between opposites. I thought I'd always realized the difference between opposites and the fine line between mindfulness and mindlessness, apathy and curiosity, reasonableness and unreasonableness, and millions of other opposites, life and death, awareness and unawareness, tolerance and intolerance, war and peace, etc. But, heretofore, that was only knowledge.

With the epiphany, I became aware that my former knowledge was more intellectual and academic rather than a deep understanding. We've all heard phrases such as, *"He's crossed the line!"* Of course I knew if a person had crossed the line, he had to have moved beyond what was appropriate. Now I know it is only reasonable that he had crossed the line between his/her own opposites, such as when a habit became an addiction, or when swiping a pen becomes shoplifting, or gossip moved across the line and became an expression of jealousy. I recently realized all these things have a fine line between what is one thing and what is altogether another.

Recently I've become amazed at how often the fine line between opposites occurs. For instance, I've always considered myself a generous, compassionate person, but since I've not yet donated money to the refugees of Syria escaping their war torn communities, I'm in the position of having to adjust my self-concept. There is still time to redeem myself by what *"I'm gonna do"*, but we all know that *"gonna do"* and *"have done"* are two different things.

So far, I've crossed my own fine line negatively between compassion and lack of caring, and that brings up another point. The awareness of the fine line between opposites applies to each individual in the world and those are as different as fingerprints. Therefore, what the fine line between opposites ultimately means, is that each person has their own fine lines between opposites that have nothing to do with another's fine lines between opposites.

There are hunters who shoot birds, deer, rabbits coyotes and wolves, and a host of other animals. Where it's against my save-the-wilderness nature to kill these living miracles, hunter's evidently have no such fine line.

Where is the fine line between tolerance and intolerance? Where is my tolerance for the American hunters, or hunters of any type, the war in Syria, health care reform, the religions of the world, abortion, pollution of air and sea, etc.? It turns out that one's fine line between opposites is alive and well differently for every human being, minute by minute, day by day, and year by year. But along the way, it's extremely important to know where I stand, and were I a preaching sort of person, I'd also recommend it be important for everyone to be aware of their own fine line and give some thought to keeping it or changing it.

I didn't say the epiphany of realizing the fine line between opposites was easy, but I'm aware that the fine line is one of the basic points for all humanity and along with tolerance, is a permanent reality to which it is incumbent we all make friends.

FEAR DREAM 78

(Yes, Harold is dreaming again. He says dreams are as much a reality as reality. Do you believe him, trust him, have confidence or faith in him?)

At the bottom of the hill
my friend grasped his umbrella.
    It became a light metal frame
    and caught the gusting wind.
Up he went, almost aloft,
    legs clipping the tops
    of tall green grass.
    Skittering up the hill,
he reached the knoll and fell,
    sprawling and falling,
    over the dry grass slope
    until the hill broke away,
    and he rode the crumbling earth,
    head protruding,
    as he would a breaking wave.
The earth-wave broke
    and swallowed him whole.
If I could not save him
    he would be buried.
I ran to the mounding pile
    of still earth.
Where shall I dig?
How would I feel
    in the heavy blackness
    unable to breathe?

ETERNITY

(Harold has a special view of life on this heaven-like planet. He thinks that all living things shall be equal in the eyes - if they have any - of the universal creative forces. Is he wrong?)

Before I begin the day's work, it is my habit to go jog-walking in the morning five days a week. I went this morning, worked up a sweat, thought about things that needed thinking about and finished in the leisurely time of 48 minutes and 35 seconds. Then I did a few arm exercises, bracing my arms against a railing and doing thirty inclined push-ups. Afterwards I took ten-pound weights in each hand and curled them sixty times, swinging them overhead every five curls. When I finished, my arms and chest were pumped up and I felt big, powerful and capable.

But while I was doing the curls I noticed a little black dot moving slowly and quietly across the concrete slab. It was a little larger than a spec and moved only two to four inches during my exercising. I wondered what kind of creature was way down there while I was way up here swinging my arms. What kind of life did it lead? It wasn't an ant or fly or spider; just a tiny black dot moving hesitantly but steadily in what seemed a totally arbitrary direction. Was it looking for food? Was it taking a little walk? Did it really have any idea why in heavens name it found itself on my concrete slab making its trip to nowhere while I exercised. Slowly it passed a hairline crack, then made its laborious way around a little piece of dirt.

When I finished my curling and arm lifts I had to have a better look at this living dot so I leaned way down from my great height and put my hands on my knees and nose within a foot of the living thing and discovered it was a beetle with an oblong shell and an abundance of almost invisible feet.

Its feelers projected a millimeter in front, wavering slightly as the beetle moved its timeless way. The bug was as alert as any bug can be and taking great care to maneuver perfectly on his journey to get where it was going.

I thought about smashing him to a pulp - a spot on the pavement – no big deal. I had just finished reading Barbara Tuchman's *A Distant Mirror,* a history of the 14th century about the chivalry of knights galloping swiftly to battle in full armor astride magnificent horses with lances and swords and bludgeons. I thought of the cheapness of life in those times and had read about never-ending wars, backbreaking taxes, and tortuous punishments during the era of the black plague. From the bug's standpoint I might have been an armored knight on a leaping horse or a seasoned warrior with a thirst for blood. If I crushed him, in the larger scheme of things, what difference would it make? Then I thought if I was crushed by a real knight what difference would that make? If we, the bug and I, were each crushed, in the larger scheme of things, it would make no difference.

As I watched him move I caught a glimpse of eternity. This harmless creature existed right in front of me not knowing how he got in to this world, yet doing something nature carefully designed him to do; living and making decisions for reasons completely unknown to me. And here I was, existing and making my way through the world, with reasons just as completely foreign to him; going about my business as nature designed me to do. I wasn't any more aware of why I was in this world than he. The beetle and I were the same. It was our job to do things nature had designed us to do. So I decided to be here and do what I was designed to do including jog-walking, exercising, laughter, sadness, catching glimpses of eternity and having all the other human strengths and frailties. Relative to his world the beetle was doing the same. I love the bug.

BECOMING WHOLE

Now that the intrepid adventurer
has dimmed the light
of youthful ardor
and has begun his advancing
in crazy swirls,
limp like a hand,
solid like a fist,
and the moons of Orion
are spilling their silvery light,
slow motion, into the emptiness,
to bathe the eyes of wonder,
stimulate the mind,
and wake the dormant heart,
I feel those gentle hands,
with billowing sleeves,
lifting my feelings
of reality,
and peace,
and love,
into the strong light
of truth,
as I become whole.

TRUST

(For the last few years Harold has needed to figure out the meaning of the word "trust." He believes if he writes down an honest interpretation of any meaningful word, it then becomes his belief. Afterward, in a discussion with anyone who cares, he has a starting place or benchmark for greater knowledge.)

TRUST is feeling certain something will happen. Like TRUST the sun will come up in the morning because it's done that for 4-1/2 billion years. There's no money to be made on a bet it won't come up.

I can also say that I have FAITH the sun will come up each morning, but FAITH and TRUST are a lot ALIKE. As a matter of fact we might as well throw in as well CONFIDENCE the sun will come up and BELIEF the sun will come up. They're practically all the same anyway, but our subject is TRUST.

It's easy to TRUST the sun coming up and easy to TRUST I will get wet when it rains, or TRUST I will get burned when my hand is in the fire, but how about marginal aspects, like a friend says, *"Hey, Buddy, let's take this shortcut!"*

You say, *"I don't feel you know where you're going and I'm not your Buddy!"*

He says, *"TRUST ME!"* Well, that blows it for sure! I'll no more trust this pigeon than I can throw an iron bathtub. His track record is not as good as the sun's coming up or my getting wet when it rains or getting a burned hand in the fire! Didn't he forget to pay me back for the money he borrowed from me twelve times? Trust HIM? Absurd! I'd rather stick my hand in a rattler hole.

Obviously, there's a lack of TRUST there, but being on a self-destructive kick and, heck without anything else to do anyway, I decide to go along with him and against my better judgment just this one last time and grudgingly

TRUST him.

As I suspected in an hour or so later, I find myself shoulder-deep in mustard weed looking for a lost bunny trail that's already split in fifteen different directions. He'd done it to me again! I'll never, never listen to him again. He looks at me, shrugs his shoulders and says, *"Ha! Ha! Ha! I'm sorry!"* I'm in a rage! TRUST has again been broken! I never TRUSTED him. I don't TRUST him! I have lost FAITH in him! I have no CONFIDENCE in him! I no longer BELIEVE in him! I have been struck once more on the back of the head with a baseball bat! I should have my head examined!

And so I have one instance of a group of reliable things: sun, rain, fire, I can TRUST, and in the other instance an example of a relationship in which TRUST, at least in the other's sense of direction, has been severely tried. Think about that for a while as I go on to something else.

The degree to which I TRUST others can be highly related to the degree to which I TRUST myself. Not TRUSTING me! Not having CONFIDENCE in me! Not BELIEVING in me and not having FAITH in me is DETRIMENTAL to me. Without those things, I'm prone to put TRUST in the hands of others.

Take the teacher-pilot, for instance, since he TRUSTS himself that he can correct major student errors and bring the plane to a safe landing, he can teach while I have CONFIDENCE in him. If the teacher-pilot feels he cannot correct student errors and bring the plane to safety, the idea of going up with a student pilot, *(me)* is abhorrent!

Pity the poor student trying to learn from a pilot who has no TRUST, FAITH, CONFIDENCE or BELIEF in himself.

Get the picture?

The next essay, and it's a tough one and I probably won't do it anyway, is **HOW to TRUST YOURSELF!**

(This, I know nothing about.)

A PROTESTATION OF THE HIGHEST ORDER

Within this attitude
of mass assassination,
let us begin to realize
the carelessness
of this numbing act
and come, for once,
to terms
with beauty,
joy and thought,
and use our gifts,
intelligence,
and boldness of spirit,
to reject
this murdering
and mayhem
in all its grim
absurdity,
and be resolved
to think instead,
on life,
awareness of women,
and sexual gratification
as the profundity
to best elicit
that self-control
over those basest
interior emotions,
and stop annihilation
in its tracks
before this horrid
specter
eliminates us all.

I cry this out
from my lofty
vantage point
with heartfelt hope
to instigate
within each breast
a will to peace,
nobility and sex.
Let us <u>all</u> hold these thoughts.

Be free!

LIFE AFTER DEATH'S OK IF YOU SURVIVE
(There comes a time in life when at the age of eighty-five, an indifferent head, "death," appears. Harold's life is 8/9 over - unless he lives longer. At best, it's eighty percent over and necessary to consider the rest of his life in relation to its end. But, like the song, "Who Knows Where or When?"

I am 99 and 44/100 percent certain there is NO life after death. There's a .56/100 percent chance there IS an afterlife and because I consider myself a percentage kind of guy and even though I see no proof of life after death, I keep a low percentage of doubt allowing myself to claim an open mind, even though, perhaps, I may not have one.

This year *(2016)*, I've read the neurologist's book called <u>*Proof of Heaven,*</u> wherein, through a rare brain disease, the doctor's cerebral cortex became completely dead, thereby convincing him his visions of the afterlife were real; and about a child of four in the book called <u>*Heaven is for Real,*</u> a book about an ailing child who has a near-death experience. He saw diseased relatives and Jesus in the afterlife and came back convinced there really, really is a heaven. I've also read two of Michael Newton's books called <u>*Journey of Souls*</u> and <u>*Destiny of Souls*</u> and found them especially fascinating. In his lifetime career, he put many people under regressive hypnosis to a point before they were born and to a place called *"between lives"* and questioned them on their past lives. I admire him because he's obviously very intelligent, experienced, and extremely explicit in his detailed reports on what his clients have to say.

But I can't seem to escape the fact that all the stories in all the life-after-death books are told when the subjects are still alive. If they didn't completely die, how can they speak of a life after death? If they were NEAR death, that means they were NOT DEAD yet, but ALMOST dead. If the heart stops for a short period of time, they are technically dead - but not so long as to be really and truly dead. I've seen road kill. There's no doubt about anything run over by a truck. They're definitely out of this world!

My dad died in 1976 and if he came back in 1977 and told me about life after death, I guess I'd have to rethink my premise. Of course, he was cremated. My mother, brother and I took the urn, gathered the warm, powdery bones, and scattered them to the Colorado winds. But I ask you, even though he was cremated, does that make a difference? Are the rules such that the body has to return to the earth from inside a coffin? Yes! I know! It makes no difference what happens to the dead body, it's only a vehicle, anyway. It's the soul that counts!

If I were to dig up a corpse after a year or so, there wouldn't be much left of the body, just some bones with yucky stuff attached. When mummy's were exhumed from the pyramids, except in funny movies, they were still unequivocally dead. None came alive and mumbled something like, *"Howdy Doody Everybody! Guess what? I'm here! Ha! Ha! I came back from the dead! Let me tell you about it."* My dad used to say the best place to bury a dead body was under a new tree. The body would decay, turning to worms and germs and whatever and would provide fertilizer.

Which brings up the point that people sometimes say, *"There is no death! Life continues! We're all ONE! We don't die, but live on and on - throughout eternity!"* Well, *"Duh!"* You're right! First you're a person, then you die, and then you come back LIVING - as worms and germs and whatever. I never seem to be able to get through to people, that life as a PERSON is what stops, not ALL LIFE EVERYWHERE!

It goes from LIFE AS A PERSON to LIFE AS WORMS AND GERMS AND WHATEVER. There's a big difference between humans and fertilizer, though, be it said, and I'll admit and agree, both ARE alive, and life DOES continue. But please admit, life as fertilizer is NOT life as human!

Then there's the condition of STRATA. Poem by me, *"In a single click of the cosmic clock, I'm STRATA!"* That means in a very short span of geologic time, I will have gone from a living, breathing, thinking, feeling, person, to a solid chunk of sedimentary rock. Of course we're talking about my body, here. But, evidently, in a few million years my dead body, like the dinosaurs, will be cast in stone. *"AHA!,* you say, *but your soul lives beyond."* And I might say, *"How do you know?"* I'm sure that humans have a collective unconscious, but is that what we're talking about? My soul becomes part of the collective unconscious! OK! I'll go with that. But were does that leave me? Other than the collective unconscious including every human that's ever lived, where does my personal, one-of-a-kind Harold fit into this picture? Where is poor little-ol'-me, in all this?

My wife says, "Remember, you leave behind lots of good architectural works, books, and artwork, all of which are influencing people, hopefully, in a positive way. When you pass on, your kids will still love and remember the good things about you and the good things you taught them." That is, after you're gone, when you've bitten the weenie, when you return to dust, when you go to never-never land, your kids will still have been influenced by you in a positive way and love you. Well, I love that! I really do!

After all, I love my mother and father, don't I? And my mother and father loved their parents, didn't they? Yes, of course, but who will love my mother and father when I'm gone? Even now, my grand kids don't know who my parents were and I know very little about my own parents before I was born. They were people of the early century. I am a person of the later century. My grand kids are a product of a new century. Times change. People change. The world population has doubled since 1980. Other than the miraculous qualities inherent in the great collective unconscious, I can't see how my grandparents are influencing anybody for the better - or for the worse, for that matter.

The truth is, nobody gets out of life alive. Besides this one-of-a-kind planet, I see no other place to go. When life is over, it's over. Kaput! Washed up! Done! Complete. Been there! Done that! When I die, I will have lived my whole life. After I'm dead, it would be great to mourn the passing of my life, but since that's impossible I must mourn it NOW. I must notice the miracles of this life - NOW!

Wherever I find it, I must be aware of my good fortune. In my life, I must accept the good and come to terms with the bad and realize it's my own personal, one-of-a-kind life that only I could have lived; that the good and the bad in my life were the only life I could have led. Like Sinatra's, I DID IT MY WAY, I'd have to say, life was good. I had great parents, went to college, got married, had three marvelous children, am now living superbly. I've had a creative career in architecture and after retirement, had a second life in art, music, and literature. In my second marriage I've shared my life with a marvelous, loving, creative, intellectual person and wouldn't trade my situation for the world. I'm happy now and when I die I will have lived a complete life with no regrets and a feeling of great joy that I was able to be part of this unending, inexplicable miracle. I could write an entire essay on the good that has happened in my life. The mistakes I've made could only have been made by me. If I hadn't made them, I wouldn't be me. So, as my mother would say, *"There you have it!"*

THE WOLF AND I

The close growl of a wolf.
The yellow, slit eye, calm gaze of the wolf.
The raised hair on the back of the neck.
The snarl and white teeth
yellowing nearer the gum-line,
vivid, as in a dream!
God, I hate that mouth!

And the patterned,
thick fur on the collar of his neck.
"What is it you want, wolf?"
I meet that steady look,
the energy pulsing forward then relaxing.
I say to the wolf, "Go away from me!"

A low growl!
Crouching, I wait.
"What are you waiting for, wolf?"
Will you eat me now, or while I sleep?
Will you chase me in the misty dawn,
through fresh green grasses,
wet with dew,
or through long primeval grasses,
headlong, in panic
with razor edges that, as I run,
lacerate my shins.

Shall I briefly register your haunches
that while you run,
flex and bunch beneath
that luxurious fur,
pursuing your prey (me)

to our final trapping place?
And with all avenues of escape exhausted,
shall I then finally pivot, in my great fear
and, surprised at finding inner strength
I knew not I had,
shall I turn, snarling,
to meet your face -
face to face?

Turn and meet your yellow teeth, my death,
as they clench and grip, and rip,
hot around my throat?
And shall you win, then,
summoning every inner resource,
or shall I somehow prevail?

Might I not, under such a threat,
get bigger than I am
and become, myself, a threat;
shoot the energy, (my will),
so forcefully from my heart and chest,
arm and teeth,
that my newfound strength
shall penetrate your hide like x-rays
that dampen your will
sending chills of your own fear descending in
waves down your yellow spine?

Or shall we clash in mortal battle as equals,
each determined to prevail?
And what of our courage, you and I?

Shall you be defeated, or I?
I'll wrench your limb from it's socket,

as you chew my forearm.
I'll plunge my fist past your yellow teeth
into your windpipe,
feeling your gagging tongue,
and so, your victim chokes <u>*you*</u>*.*
You'll roll back your eyes,
and with claws extended,
whip and undulate your body
in a frantic effort to free yourself.
And wolf, with slit eyes,
focused, intent,
locked in steady contact on mine,
who watches us struggle?

Does our maker sit,
white-robed,
enthralled upon the spectacle?
Perhaps enjoying or lamenting
the spectacle of his (our) conflict?
Does he sit alone on his golden throne
(with selected angels)
conducting a test of wills-to-survive?
Or is there no maker?
All gone home.
(An empty throne.)
No one watching.
Bleachers bare,
while we combat for no reason?

Is there no way to make peace,
you and I,
yellow, slit-eyed wolf,
with determined gaze,
fixed eyes , steady, on mine?

*If so, we must relax simultaneously
and find mutual trust.*

If so, what an invincible team we'd be!

HAROLD'S CONCERNS

(Harold firmly believes there should be no process without being in context and that if concern for all living beings on our miraculous planet is an important issue, education is at the top of the list. Here are a few things with which he thinks humans should be concerned.)

One! - Health of our planet.

It bothers me that even though we can record history, write books, build airplanes, rocket to the Moon, build cyclotrons, highway systems, huge buildings, etc., we can't control our human sexuality that is resulting in an extremely severe population explosion. At the present humans are unable to quit cutting down forests, stop polluting air and oceans, damming rivers, poisoning our food, using up our natural resources, etc., etc.

If all the animals, birds, reptiles, fish, mollusks, insects, crocodiles, elephants, lions, tigers, bears, whales, porpoises, yes, and even germs like Ebola and the AIDS virus, yes and even bigfoot, were the only inhabitants on the planet, it would be better off. The dinosaurs ruled the planet for 135 million years, unable to pollute the air, destroy the ocean or clear the forests. To show the immense amount of time of life of the dinosaurs as compared to the time since Jesus Christ died, consider the following proportions: Two thousand thirteen years since the time of Christ is .000015 percent of the length of time the dinosaurs dominated the planet. Think of the planetary damage humans have done to the planet in the last hundred years.

At Christ's birth the world population was between two and three-hundred million people which only equals one-fifth to one-third of one-billion. The world population is now 7.4 billion and rapidly producing a world catastrophe in food and water. The Acid Sea of Reality plainly shows us that humans are the worst planetary disease imaginable. While the world population increases with a horrendous acceleration, there seems nothing I can personally do to stop it. And so as a person with family and friends occupying a microscopic place on earth, I have to accept the population explosion and put it down as FATE. In the meantime, all that's left to do after desperate prayer and keeping my powder dry by joining all the helpful organizations of which I'm economically capable, is find the more enjoyable aspects of this miraculous, heaven-like planet upon which I am so fortunate to live and enjoy them to the best of my ability.

Two! - Earth as everyone's mother!
The inability of humans seemingly to understand that our only miraculous, mother-planet gave birth, solely, to everything on it, which means to destroy anything on it including plants, animals, birds, fish, trees, bushes, flowers, serpents, whales, including any habitat that provides a place for life, is to destroy one of our brothers and sisters and the environment which gives them life.

Yes! It's a fact that everything that lives has to kill certain living beings to stay alive, and the living beings have to accept that as FATE and abide by the rules or die. I can accept that! I like a fish sandwich as well as anyone else. What I object to is the willful killing of anything alive except for those essentials which would limit the food and water necessary to keep me alive. In other words, I think the people of the planet should be judicious when killing for food. The unnecessary scraping of the bottom of the ocean and ruining the birthplace and habitat of edible crustaceans, or the corrupt use of pesticides, or killing shark for fins, or elephants or rhinoceroses for their tusks, is unthinking and immoral. There's got to be a better way to survive.

Three! - Religious and other competitions of the world. According to a reliable source on the Internet, religions fall into six major categories:

> *Christians -   32.00%*
> *Muslims -   23.00%*
> *Non-religious - 13.00%*
> *Hindus -   14.00%*
> *Others -   11.00 % (includes Judaism)*
> *Buddhists -   7.00 %*

Christianity and the Muslims are the two largest religions in the world. According to the media and general theory, there is a vast difference in thinking between the two religions. As I understand it, with the exception of Iran and some of Iraq, there is minimal opportunity for education in most of the Muslim countries. There seems an extreme lack of employment, much poverty, and less than equal treatment of women. In Saudi Arabia, I understand, women are not allowed to drive and do the simplest things outside the home without being escorted by a male, apparently of any age.

The middle eastern Muslim fundamentalists, that erroneously seem to the people of the United States to represent the whole of the Muslim religion, made an attack on the predominately Christian United States. *(Muslims attack Christians)* On September 11, 2001, the two, 110 story World Trade Center towers and a good portion of the Pentagon were destroyed and almost 3,000 people lost their lives. This prompted an attack by the United States, right or wrong, on Iraq, presumably as one of the countries harboring nuclear devices, but also of ridding Iraq of the notorious Saddam Hussein and the suspected Osama Bin Laden's terrorist organization. After a ten-year war eliminating Saddam and finding no nuclear devices or any of Osama Ben Laden's organizations, the correctness of the invasion will long be debated. It changed Iraq's political and religious structure from Sunni to Shia instituting what can only be called a religious war within the same country.

Is the country's Christian power system, then, at war with the Muslim power system? Can there be tolerance and understanding where there is such a different point of view? Who is the better educated? Who is better prepared militarily? How can such predominately poor countries get a deeper education? It's obvious they can't get it by reading just one book - the Quran?

Four! - Nuclear war.
Consider the proliferation of nuclear warheads!
Those countries participating in the Non-Proliferation Treaty:

Country	Average number of nuclear warheads
USA	5,075
Russia	5,900
United Kingdom	192
France	295
China	240

Those countries not in the Non-Proliferation Treaty:

India	90
Pakistan	100
North Korea	10
Israel	140 Undeclared

Fortunately, the second highest military preparedness is the United States, which is predominately Christian.

The Christians have the guns and by average are better educated. Much less so, the Middle East. The Muslims have no guns, but fundamentalists are devious, kind of like the American Indians hiding and lying in wait to ambush both Republicans and Democrats. Is, then, our present cold war between two religions a number of countries against one big one, one of which has the big guns and the other more or less educationally poverty stricken? Is the disparity between two ways of seeing life; two ways of establishing power; two areas of the world whose idea of life are different? The solution: Education. What about North Korea and Iran? Will they make good their threats on developing nuclear power? Will deliverable nuclear bombs fall into fundamentalist hands? What can I do to protect my wife and family? More FATE?

Five! - World population
Mankind has been around for about a million years. At the time of Christ, the nearest estimates of world population were between 250 and 300 million people. It didn't start significantly growing until the early eighteenth century. Thereafter, it began its exponential growth. As late as 1980, the world reached well over three billion people.

Since 1980 *(thirty-seven years)*, it has more than doubled. In March of 2012, it reached over seven billion people. Experts estimate it will grow at about 1.5 percent every year. Today it's four-tenths over seven billion people.

There are various estimates of growth increases and decreases until the year 2100. Some say it will increase to sixteen billion, others say it will decrease to six billion. It remains to be seen, but the Acid Sea of Reality tells us the more people, the less natural resources to maintain them. Already there is a shortage of water for the thirsts and needs of a huge quantity of humanity. The toll on forests, the need for gas and oil and the necessity of *"fracking,"* which scares the heck out of me because of the extreme likelihood of contaminated groundwater.

To get an idea of the world population at the time of Christ in relation to the present population, if, two thousand years ago, the number of people could be housed within the dimensions of a square five yards at one corner of a football field, it would require an entire football field and a half to accommodate the rest of today's world population.

Rather than continue to mop up the mess, it's necessary we turn off the faucet. I know there are organizations attempting to do that and they are organizations to which I'm inspired to donate. I applaud them heartily.

Six! - Education:
I'd love it if all nations had grammar schools, high schools, universities and places of higher education. Educational facilities are the flowers of any nation. When a country matures, they flower with education. I would that all nations be filled with bouquets of flowers. It's sad when a country is so poor it doesn't have schools or methods of higher education. Countries with schools are an indication of a country that values learning, hence, a country or nation of knowledge. In my exaggerated thinking about the ultimate results of thinking good or bad, knowledge equals life, ignorance equals death. First the flower then the seed! The seeds of educational flowers are the source of mighty trees. Schools utilize the right side of the brain for ideas and creativity, the left side for reasoning and bringing those ideas into reality. The right side tells us WHAT to do and the left IMPLEMENTS WHAT to do! I'm reminded of one of a portion of T. S. Eliot's poem called, *The Hollow Men:*

Between the desire

And the spasm
Between the potency
And the existence
Between the essence
And the descent
Falls the Shadow

Simplified, it means between the desire and the reality falls the shadow. Thinking of the idea is different than bringing the idea into existence. They are two different phases.

If the desire is to regain a healthy planet, the left brain will tell us HOW to bring it into existence. The shadow is no education, no ideas, no dealing with the execution of the ideas. People of the planet must deal with the shadow.

Seven! - Light

Light travels at 186,000 miles per second. In one year, light would travel 5,865,696,000,000 miles; *(5 trillion, 865 billion, 696 million miles).* The nearest star, Alpha Centauri, is 4.3 light years away and it is doubtful it has an inhabitable planet. The North Star is 300 light-years away. If one inch equals a million miles, Alpha Centauri world be over 400 miles away. If people travel in a space ship at 25,000 miles per hour, it would take 10,000 years to reach the nearest star, Alpha Centauri. WE ARE ALONE!

Eight! - Time

Time: As far as humans are concerned, time is a straight line. The earth was formed about 4.5 billion years ago and for four billion years it was basically cooling and dormant. A billion years is 1 with 9 zeros after it. A million is one with 6 zeros after it. A thousand is 1 with 3 zeros after it. 2.016 thousand years ago was the birth of Christ. Relating 2.016

thousand years ago to one million years is to take 2.016 divided by 1,000,000, or in time, roughly two-millionths years. In other words, in relation to geologic time, humans haven't been here very long, especially when compared to that of dinosaurs that lived here for 135 million years. The lesson: Time elapsed since the birth of Christ may be significant in terms of our lives, but in terms of the planet's life it is the thickness of a coat of paint on the top floor of the new World Trade Center.

Nine! - Distance:

Solid objects in our universe are so far away, scientists measure them in light years. The moon is almost 239,000 miles away and it takes light a little over a second for it to reach the earth. The sun is almost 93,000,000 miles away and it takes light about 8.32 minutes to reach the earth. A light year is the distance a beam of light will travel in a vacuum in one year at 186,000 miles per second. In one year light travels almost six trillion miles. A trillion is 1,000,000,000,000.

The distance to the nearest star, Alpha Centauri, is 4.24 light years or 25.44 trillion miles. That's more than 25 times the distance from earth to sun. IF there is a life-giving planet orbiting around Alpha Centauri and a similar distance to the earth's distance from our sun, and IF it is a metal based sun and planet, and IF it had sufficient water and IF the period of living development could develop a thinking, feeling, creative spirit like ours, and IF they could send off a space ship or two to visit the earth at the rate of 25,000 miles an hour, it would take 112,492.8 years to get here and by then we'd probably all be dead. Let's face it. In the ACID SEA OF REALITY, we are not going to escape and we are not going to be invaded by weird looking aliens.

Ten! - Our privileged planet position.

Our huge moon is sufficiently close to stabilize the normal wobble of our planet. If our planet had no moon, it would wobble to such a degree that tides, depending on the terrain, would extend hundreds of miles inland twice a day and life like ours might never have come about. The close proximity of our large moon stabilizes the severe wobble of our planet.

The earth is virtually inundated with water that creates tides and circulation, rainstorms, evaporation, condensation, clouds, hurricanes and typhoons. The earth is close enough to the sun that because of gravity, water not only seeps into cracks, but freezes and expands, breaking rocks, and continually forcing minerals and metallic elements into the atmosphere that are critical to all life. The underwater seepage from the interior of our planet into the center of our oceans eventually forces land masses to contact the edge of continents creating volcanoes that spew molten metal, steam, lava, and life enhancing minerals into the atmosphere, thereby enriching and benefitting the earth. *(Ring of Fire)*

If these facts are universally internalized by all the humans on our planet, the ultimate realization would be to know this is the only planet we will ever have and no one from outer space is going to save us. This earth is the only heaven to be realized, because the only other alternative is an eternity of unconsciousness. The soul is connected to the body. Without the body, there is no soul. When the body dies, the soul dies. By being born on this earth, we've won the prize and possibly for the first time we can see that it's good and do our best to keep the good and try our damnedest to eliminate the bad.

ON BEING FREE
(Hal finally tells us who he wants to be and what he wants to do.)

I run through forests
racing trunks
on needles
soft as down.

I leap branches,
jump streams,
hurtle stones.
I run with perfect ease
and grace
in perfect time,
and perfect rhythm,
for I am a man with
a perfect purpose.

I am clouds and sky,
wild yellow roses
in tall green grass,
a lover of food and sleep,
women and song.

I run like the wind
combing the field
on some black night
and never am tired.

I am infinite variety,
leaves on the tree,
feathers on the wing,

scales in the murk
of some lost sea.
I never stop inhaling.
My lungs are big as buildings.
I only breathe out when I want
and that for purest pleasure.

I am big and free,
long of arm,
long of torso,
hip and thigh.

I swim oceans,
climb mountains.
I fly through the air,
and sing with birds.

I love it here.
It's made for me,
my world.
It has infinite variety.

I rise and float.
I sing a two day song.
I play if I want
for as long as a year,
and never get tired.

I am a meteoric boulder,
pea-sized,
tumbling in a shallow stream.

I lie in wait for a year
or doze and dream,

perfectly content.

Darkness doesn't bother me,
nor does the desert air.
Mighty rainstorms are my home.
I wish they'd never end,
for I have time.

I do not age,
but seemingly grow younger
with every passing day.

The pathway clears itself before me.
Giant pines move their trunks
to avoid my stride.
Mountains open as I approach,
and when I'm gone,
close themselves behind.

I wade the seas
and visit islands.
The sea turtle is my friend.
We swim together,
arm and fin,
in silent harmony.

I follow the whale
to hidden depths
and linger just a while.

I sift my fingers
through silts of ages
in the pitch of the Japanese trench.

I calibrate the shifts
of continental plates
before I go to lunch.
I marvel at a grain of sand
glistening in the sun.
Or a quiet tear.
Or a drop of dew.
Or a raindrop,
cool and clear.

I love my private world,
and my perfect purpose.
The purpose of being.

WE SHALL
(Will you, then, be faithful to me as I have been to you?)

It is my deepest concern, for without you the world
would crumble to dust and molten lava and stones would
spew forth into eternity's great cavern never to return.
See this, sweet one, worry not. I love you and faith in each
other is a powerful bridge leading to promised lands.

I love you and this is the source of my strength. The
tree grows stalwart to heaven, pink and red with sap, it
blooms hello as does the shark moving slowly through
great depths.

We wish and are fulfilled if only we see the light. Shrimp
glimmer beneath the surface as unanswered questions.

Keen am I on this place and long to know all there is
and long to grow. The blade of grass bends and waves,
living beneath the cool wind and sky. I see you, clouds,
drifting to your place to evaporate and die. Over ocean
or land, somewhere you cease to exist as we all must.

This interlude is but a stretch of heaven to get us by until
the next heaven. I shall return as a salamander enjoying
the cool, leafy water and bury myself in the muck of the
cool sweet earth. There I shall breathe and breed; spew
forth my flowering sperm and sow my oats upon rich lands
and procreate, for that is what I do. That is my purpose.
That is what makes my heart leap with joy. That is my
fullest expression of the love of being. That is my gift to
the universe and as I have been given this gift shall strive
to give my gift.

That which makes my heart sing shall be my gift
and I shall accept as my right, freedom, as the wind
surrounds the planet, gathers in storms and hurricanes
or blows a zephyr across the desert wild-flowers, pure,
simple and infinitely renewed by the freshness of the

vast waters and growing things; cleaned and furrowed by the sharp and glistening points of mountains, I shall, as the wind, be free.

As the wind, I shall find my power, my strength in sensitivity and appreciation. In love I shall live and give. See here now, this is the way to live! To grow! To be!

Won't the air be ridden with thunderstorms and stabbed with lightning bolts? Won't hurricanes hurl throngs of saltwater droplets at the seashore towns and cities? Won't the Payne's Gray underbelly of the clouds in its vastness be spectacular? Won't the immense cloud light up and glow from its interior with curved gray shadows, giving it form, volume and dimension?

Shan't we be part of this natural force and feel its being as our own? We shall!

ACKNOWLEDGEMENTS

I want to thank Helane Freeman for her tireless work in getting this book edited and printed through Ingram/ Sparks printing company, facilitating requirements for ISBN numbers and sales by Amazon. I'd like to thank Jack Birdsall, now deceased, for his long hours of work editing, organizing and getting this book published the first time with LULU publishing company. I'm grateful to Ron Munro who started me on WordStar many years ago and regularly continues to improve my understanding of the computer and its use. Thanks to Tom Rincker, computer professional and owner of Applications Recording, who is continually available to assist me in keeping my computer running. I wish to thank my loving wife, Marge, mother, therapist, dancer, and artist, recently retired as a twenty-seven year Grief Counselor at the Thousand Oaks, California, Hospice of the Conejo. I love her helpful suggestions and objective views of what I've written and for her solid stance behind me, my ideas, and all my written activities. And I'd like to thank my three adult children and four step-children and their spouses, and eight beautiful and intelligent grandchildren for encouraging me in all my endeavors.

Appreciatively, *Doug*

OTHER BOOKS BY DOUG RUCKER

Personal Journey	Poem & Prose. A journey through Doug's divorce.
Early Stories	Autobiography – Volume 1 - Birth through University.
Groundwork	Autobiography – Volume 2 - Marriage through Malibu architectural office.
Moving Through	Collection of 400 + pages of poems and 22 *"No Think"* pastels.
Growing Edge	Autobiography - Early architectural practice including pedestal house.
Book of Words	Collection of 69 essays - humor and philosophy.
Reflections	Art book - 25 color reflection photos with text.
Where's the Cookies At?	Silly stories and poems by Roy Crandal.
Off the Wall	Art book with 24 abstract, colored photos based on Graffiti.

BRIEF BIOGRAPHY

After finishing eighth grade in Chicago, Illinois, Doug was awarded a scholarship to the Chicago Art Institute. Entering Austin High School, he had a wonderful time in athletics and pursued a three-year college preparatory course in architecture. At the Champaign-Urbana University of Illinois he took a Bachelor of Science degree in architecture and afterward worked as a draftsman in Denver and San Diego. In Pasadena he married his first wife and received his California Architectural License.

In a house of his own design in Santa Monica Canyon, his first wife, Karon, gave birth to three marvelous daughters and in 1966 he built his own Malibu *"dream house"*, the forty-two foot square main floor floating on a twenty-six foot square pedestal thirty-five feet in the air with a wrap-around deck and spectacular views of the ocean, estuary, Malibu Movie Colony and Surfrider Beach. He received much newspaper and magazine notoriety before it was burned to the ground late in 1970. By 1972 he'd built another more fire-resistant and equally dramatic house over the same foundations. It was similarly honored and published - but lost to a divorce in 1980.

He and Marge, his new wife of thirty years, are enjoying the creative life in a very small house of his own design on an acre of land in the mountains six miles above Malibu. Semi-retired, he's enjoying writing books and showing his photographic art in galleries.

www.ingramcontent.com/pod-product-compliance
Lightning Source LLC
Chambersburg PA
CBHW071856090426
42811CB00004B/637